The Persecuted Prophets

The Persecuted Prophets

KAREN W. CARDEN
ROBERT W. PELTON

South Brunswick and New York: A. S. Barnes and Company
London: Thomas Yoseloff Ltd

©1976 by A. S. Barnes and Co., Inc.

A. S. Barnes and Co., Inc.
Cranbury, New Jersey 08512

Thomas Yoseloff Ltd
108 New Bond Street
London W1Y OQX, England

Library of Congress Cataloging in Publication Data

Carden, Karen W
    The persecuted prophets.

    1. Snake cults (Holiness churches) 2. Holiness churches—
Appalachian Mountains, Southern. I. Pelton, Robert W.,
1934-   Joint author. II. Title.
BX7990.H6C28   1975   289.9   74-10322
ISBN 0-498-01511-4

PRINTED IN THE UNITED STATES OF AMERICA

Dedicated to
Estle P. Muncy, M. D.
of Jefferson City, Tennessee
An untiring, much loved country doctor. One who is the epitome
of this almost forgotten early American breed.
and to

Reverend Alfred Ball and his wife, Sister Eunice
of
Newport, Tennessee
Two extraordinarily gifted, unquestionably sincere,
and totally dedicated children of God.

Contents

7

Preface

It is more ridiculous to ridicule than to accept. What can society grant its members if not the right to believe and practice their chosen faith? Do the courts dare deny a man the opportunity to carry out the dictates of his own conscience? When uninspired men impose strict regulations and limitations upon those professing true and real spiritual contact, the whole freedom of worship concept is defeated. Non-believers should not be so vocal with their skepticism, so desperate in their condemnation, nor so dedicated to their persecution. For, having never been touched, selected, or moved in a particular manner, they simply do not know.

A man has the right to avoid what he fears; but should respect any unusual courage in another. He should cling to his personal convictions, but still maintain the generosity to let others do the same. He must decide on the ruling forces of his own mind and heart, but should not take on the burdensome responsibility of passing judgment on something he refuses to understand.

This exciting book deals with the mountain church people of the Appalachia region—those who are known to handle poisonous snakes and drink strychnine, as well as numerous other dangerous concoctions, during religious services. It is the true story of the Southeast's Holiness serpent handlers as told by the members who literally interpret and base their doctrine on the five signs found in St. Mark, Chapter 16, verses 17 and 18:

And these signs shall follow them that believe:
In my name shall they cast out devils; they shall
speak with new tongues. They shall take up serpents;
and if they drink any deadly thing, it shall not
hurt them; they shall lay hands on the sick, and
they shall recover.

Robert W. Pelton
Karen W. Carden

Meditate upon these things;
give thyself wholly to them. . .
I Timothy, 4:15

Reverend Alfred Ball handling a large rattlesnake. "If somebody beats me until I can't get up off the ground and walk off, I hope I've got enough of the grace of God to let them do it," explains Brother Ball. "I've had my face slapped and I've had enough grace to turn the other cheek. I've been choked nearly to the point of passing out. I had enough grace to take it."
Photo by Estle P. Muncy, M. D.

Acknowledgments

The authors are grateful to every person who helped make this book a reality. Our special thanks go to Alfred and Eunice Ball, Dr. Estle P. Muncy, and Richard L. Williams.

To this mention we would like to add Larry Aldridge, News Editor, *Newport Plain Talk*; Joe Anderson, WKGN News Director; Clyde Ricker; Ralph Eslinger and family; Robert Grooms; Floyd McCall and family; Kelly Williams; Ralph Spence; Danny Smith; Lester Ball; Roy James Birckhead; Willie E. Sizemore; Robert and Everett Fraley; John Brown; Billy Jay Forrester; Mary Kate Williams; Candis Williams; Ruth Dillon; Mary Bailey; Lida Davis; Thelma Whittaker; and all the other dedicated people involved either directly or indirectly with the project.

The Persecuted Prophets

1

Introducing the Persecuted Prophets

The kings of the earth set themselves, and
the rulers take counsel together, against
the Lord, and against his anointed, . . .
                              Psalms, 2:2

The Lord forbid that I should do this thing
unto my master, the Lord's anointed, to
stretch forth mine hand against him, seeing
he is the anointed of the Lord.
                              1. Samuel, 24:6

Blanket freedom to choose a particular form of worship is granted to every citizen under the Constitution of the United States:

ARTICLE I. Congress shall make no law respecting an establishment of religion, or prohibiting the free exercise thereof. . . .

Similar articles are found in each and every State Constitution. These constitutional guarantees also carry with them the freedom to not take part in any form of religious practice an individual finds distasteful. Legislation is certainly not required to safeguard John Q. Public from

15

But in the fourth generation
they shall come hither again.
Genesis, 15:16

The controversial, rather isolated one room church buried in a heavily wooded hollow on English Mountain. "We're not really interested in growing," offers Reverend Alfred Ball, the co-pastor. "The main purpose of churches who go out and knock on doors is to increase their membership. They are more interested in how many people they have in church instead of how good a Christian the people are. We would rather have ten people who were really truly born again Christians than to have 150 people who were in church just to be in church."
Photo by Larry Aldridge.

any scripturally sanctioned religious activity. Yet, fear of harm to on-lookers is the alleged basis of state laws against the persecuted funda-mentalist serpent handlers.

One of the motivating forces in the founding of America was com-plete and unrestricted religious freedom. Hence, the development of the Methodists, Baptists, Presbyterians, Lutherans, Episcopalians, Catholics, Mormons, Quakers, Seventh Day Adventists, Jehovah's Witnesses, Unitarians, Christian Scientists, Churches of God, Holiness Churches,

. . .from generation to generation.
Exodus, 17:16

Brother Danny Smith of Morristown, Tennessee, and Brother Leonard Green of Middlesboro, Kentucky. Danny is a youthful 30. Both his mother and father were serpent handlers. Danny first took up the serpent in church when he was fifteen. He then "backslid" and twelve years later, "got right with God." Brother Danny Smith took up a serpent the first Sunday he came back to the Lord and has "been doing it ever since."
Photo by Jack Hixson.

and all succeeding branches of each. This religious freedom and development is unparalleled anywhere else in the world.

Who is to say when a religious practice is endangering a nonmember? Do not some believers literally "fear" the teachings projected by others? Are not some doctrines considered "dangerous" by those who embrace other theologies? For example, there has been no legislation declaring that Catholicism puts Methodists in peril; although many of the second group feel a definite threat to their spiritual well-being. And how many Baptists have had their church doors padlocked in the face of adverse feeling?

Imagined danger gives way to real fear. People who freely choose to expose themselves to a situation look rather silly when they turn to the courts for protection. They appear even more ridiculous when the question arises—"Protection from what?" More foolish still are the initiators of religious oriented legal action when they never bother to observe first hand the activities of their church-related defendants. One such initiator is District Attorney General Henry F. "Dutch" Swann, the prosecutor in the controversial Cocke County case against the Holiness Church of God In Jesus Name, located in tiny Carson Springs, Tennessee—a case which the American Civil Liberties Union has seen fit to step into. (This case is discussed in detail in Chapter 10.)

Curiosity, ridicule, fascination, or even hearsay are hardly logical grounds for the time and expense involved in convening a grand jury, conducting hearings, holding trials, and issuing injunctions. Yet, to courtroom observers, these grounds seemed to be of much more importance than letter of the law charges.

The belief in and practice of the five signs set down in St. Mark 16:17-18[1] is the running thread that connects a large group of widespread Appalachian Holiness fundamentalists. These people zealously follow all five signs: They take up serpents; they drink various poisons; they heal the sick; they speak in unknown tongues; they cast out devils. A very few die. Most live to proclaim the "perfect victory" of God. Other doctrinal ideas and procedures differ from church to church, as is characteristic of the whole world of religion.

Serpent handling seems unusual to most people in this day of rationalized or tailor-made religions. Yet, to the participants, it is simply the carrying out of one important scriptural sign—a declaration of faith and confirmation of the Word as commanded by Jesus after the Resurrection. Furthermore, their literal interpretation of the Bible leads them to observe Communion, or the Lord's Supper, baptism by immersion, and many more of the identical examples followed by all evangelistic associations.

---

1. Interestingly enough, the same five signs are also found in the BOOK OF MORMON, Chapter 9, verse 24.

Taking up serpents isn't really so strange to the Church of God, the very Church who presently complains most vocally against the Holiness Church of God In Jesus Name. "It's almost like the pot calling the kettle black," according to one elderly brother, his leathery face breaking into a mischievous smile. Their criticism is based on the fact that the words "Church of God" are used in the name of the controversial church of serpent handlers. They seem not to wish to become tainted by reputation. Yet, this same Church of God sanctioned serpent handling as recently as 1920. Only then was it outlawed. And those who determinedly continued the practice, as numerous worshipers did, were excommunicated.

The consecrated, dedicated Holiness people of the Southeastern United States are undeniably real and unfortunately misrepresented in almost every situation. They ask *only* to be allowed to worship as they are led by God. They strive quietly but earnestly to spread the Gospel as *they* feel it should be spread. They turn with zeal and total sincerity to prayer, healing, Bible study and salvation of souls.

In the following pages you will witness the sad and frustrating court case against a little one room church on Tennessee's mountainous eastern border. This legal battle was initiated when two ardent young men of the faith died after drinking strychnine at a Saturday night service on April 7, 1973. Ironically, this act itself is not against the law; yet, it was the questionable grounds on which legal action was initiated by the state. *The Persecuted Prophets* is an important book—one that should have been written years ago. In it you will come to understand why the faithful do not milk the venom, defang, or alter their reptiles in any way. But most important of all, you will meet the people. You will listen to them speak, hear them sing, pray, preach, heal, and cast out devils. And you will watch those "anointed" take up serpents and ingest poison.

Included in these pages are eyewitness accounts of youthful Brother Buford Pack and Reverend Jimmy Williams, who, when anointed, drank strychnine and died during a recent service at a small church located at the end of a road, up a little hollow near Newport, Tennessee. Reverend Willie E. Sizemore, the pastor of the Full Gospel Jesus Church in Columbus, Ohio, who daringly handles fire and serpents, and boldly drinks large doses of strychnine during church services and revivals.

Beautiful sixteen-year-old Vicki Hoosier, who handles five foot rattlesnakes during services at the Full Gospel Jesus Church in Micco, West Virginia. The late Reverend Richard Williams of Columbus, Ohio, who, "in the name of Jesus," regularly drank strychnine, sometimes placed his bare feet in a box of curling, hissing copperheads while preaching, and picked up rattlesnakes by the handfuls. Burly Floyd McCall of Greenville, South Carolina, a man of God who often becomes anointed and gulps down unadulterated battery acid and other poisons.

...who can stretch forth his hand
against the Lord's anointed...
I Samuel, 26:9

Reverend Alfred Ball, co-pastor of the Holiness Church of God in Jesus Name, Carson Springs, Tennessee. "Strychnine has never been placed on the pulpit, and people asked to come forward and drink it," states Brother Ball in answer to some of his most vocal critics. "No one is *ever* even asked to take up serpents. They come of their *own* free will. They do it *only* because they want to—*not* because somebody has asked them to or tried to persuade them to."
Photo by Estle P. Muncy, M.D.

He, his wife, Sister Margie, and their children, take up serpents without fear. Youthful Clyde Ricker of Hot Springs, North Carolina, who was the first preacher ever to handle a deadly Indian cobra and live to tell about it. Bishop Kelly Williams of Switzer, West Virginia, who has drunk strychnine by the gallons over a period of the past twenty years.

This man still does it approximately twice weekly during church services and nightly during revivals.

Crying Danny Smith, a young man who stays in the anointed state around the clock and is ever ready to fearlessly take up the serpent. Ralph Spence, a former professional musician who takes up serpents, handles fire, and drinks strychnine. Brother Ralph, warmly referred to as the Indian by his friends in the faith, now gets his "liberty" playing his soul-stirring guitar melodies for the Lord. And slender Alfred Ball, a totally unpretentious man of God who is an untiring dynamo of religious fervor—a man with complete power over serpents, an uncanny ability to heal the sick, and a special calling to cast out devils.

These are but a few of the interesting people covered in *The Persecuted Prophets*. This book is a first! Grant yourself an open mind and a receptive heart as you read. The authors do not try to psychoanalyze those who practice this religion. They do not pass judgment. They simply present the truth and the facts regarding the Holiness serpent handlers of the Southeast.

2

A Morning of Serpent Handling

And the disciples were filled with
joy and with the Holy Ghost.
The Acts, 13:52

For every kind of beasts, and of
birds, and of serpents, and of things
in the sea, is tamed, and hath been
tamed, of mankind.
James, 3:7

The out-of-towners said it was a "homecoming." The members are
still calling it "the dinner." The news media flashed it, snapped it, and
rolled it off their presses as a "National Convention." Whatever it was
called, it was a soul satisfying day of God love and gospel rock.

The diminutive, shingled, one-room church couldn't hold them all, so
it didn't even try. It settled back in the cove and dumped its spirit-filled
contents onto the adjoining dirt parking lot and down the dusty road-
way. Uplifted palms and raised faces loudly praised God. Solemnly
bowed heads over folded hands whispered, "Thank you, Jesus." Every

child of God was praying in his own way. The faithful simply put themselves in the hands of the Lord. And the colorful band, with guitars, drums, cymbals, and tambourines, played on.

This was the scene on English Mountain near Newport, Tennessee, on Sunday, July 1, 1973. Singing, chanting, and clapping hands, Holiness serpent handlers and faithful believers from ten states had happily come together for Christian fellowship, to practice a way of worship, and for just plain good times. Automobiles streamed along the typically narrow, winding, mountain dirt road. If comers couldn't drive all the way, they simply parked their cars and walked on up.

Some folks were there looking for old friends. And some folks were there, just looking. Strangers and curiosity seekers were made to feel at home.

Newsmen, reporters, and cameramen were first welcomed, then tolerated, and finally dismissed. One preacher later explained that the confusion they produced created a "contentious spirit," and that, "Satan sent the news photographers to break the anointments."

Reverend Alfred Ball, co-pastor of the little mountain church, made it clear that outsiders were more than welcome to visit and attend services. "We want you to see and judge for yourself. We don't require people to handle the serpents. We welcome people to come to our church, no matter who they are."

Sister Nellie Pack was there. She is a slender, somewhat reserved Holiness woman who sings at all the services. Sister Nellie didn't take up any serpents during the weekend festivities, for, as she explained, "I don't handle snakes, myself." Yet, approximately six weeks later, at a prayer meeting in the home, this quiet lady forcefully received the Spirit and did take up a large hissing rattler.

There was John "Doc" Walls, a bearded professional snake exhibitor from Pensacola, Florida, who had brought some of his deadly display with him. As usual with skeptical newcomers, Walls was quick to voice his serpent handling theory. "If you leave their heads alone, you can get away with it. Faith has not one iota to do with it." The colorful Florida showman was to undergo a radical change in attitude a few hours later.

"We know these serpents are dangerous," softly explained Brother Danny Smith of Morristown, Tennessee, as he pointed to four wooden boxes of curling, hissing snakes. He and others warned the curious and the newsmen to stand back when the squirming reptiles were to be brought out of their closed containers. "We're not snake experts, and we don't handle them to show off. There's a right time to take up the serpents. That's when you're anointed."

"You should pick up the serpents only when you're under God's anointing," shouted another enthusiastic man of the faith. "I never go near them, or even try to touch one unless I feel the Holy Ghost come down on me. You've got to go and take them up in the right spirit, or they'll bite you and hurt you."

The All for Jesus Singers strummed and drummed delight into the hands and feet of the onlookers. The calm reassurance of "I Won't Have to Worry Anymore" drifted down the valley. The lively tempo of "This Little Light of Mine" reverberated off the surrounding hillsides. Sister Eunice Ball, the talented, deep-voiced young lead singer stirred the crowd with her rousing version of "Holy, Holy, Holy." While the musicians made their "joyful noise unto the Lord," there were other captivating sounds—a sinister shuffle of coiling and uncoiling copperheads in the boxes, the chilling percussion of the rattlesnakes' whirr.

A youthful, vigorous minister drew unwavering attention when he began preaching with a shoeless, sock-clad foot resting inside one of the home-made wooden boxes. Reverend Richard L. Williams of Hilliard, Ohio, firmly commanded the squirming copperheads to, "in the name of Jesus, be still!" They were. He delivered a short but spirited sermon while standing in the tangle of submissive reptiles. He was not bitten!

Brother Williams, renowned for his many triumphs of the faith, also subdued a threatening rattlesnake the same morning. He insistently thrust a forefinger at the rattler's nose and ordered it likewise to be still, "in the name of Jesus." The bewildered reptile obligingly relaxed his striking coil and rested his head on the ground. The handsome blond preacher's authority was complete. He surely had, in that spirit, "dominion. . .over every living thing that moveth upon the earth."

According to Reverend Clyde Ricker, an ordained minister from Hot Springs, North Carolina, the faithful do not smoke, drink or wear any sort of makeup. "We don't believe in putting on airs," said Brother Clyde, "each man should have a wife of his own. He shouldn't have girl friends on the side. Our women are made to wear long dresses. They do this so as not to tempt any man."

Dexter Callahan of Harlan, Kentucky, became anointed and held a home-made torch to his hands. The blaze was produced by a Pepsi bottle filled with kerosene. A thick piece of cloth was stuffed in the bottle for use as a wick. Brother Dexter's hands were blackened after he held them to the flame for over a minute. There was no apparent pain, no blistering, and even the hairs on the backs of his hands weren't singed.

Sister Nellie also handles fire. She became anointed to do this about three weeks before the homecoming. "No, it don't burn," the granny dressed woman smiled. "The only thing it does is turn my hands black and that washes right off. There aren't any blisters or any harm done because of the fire."

Brother Burl Barbee chattered like a runaway machinegun: "Some of you might think that we're here to put on a show. They say 'Look at them ol' snake handlers.' They say we're testing our faith. Bless God, we're not. We're here for Jesus. Bless God."

"You never saw any sign out front saying what we were going to do, did you?" shouted another of the eager faithful. "We don't know what

And the word of the Lord came . . .
I Kings, 21:28

A giant rattlesnake is taken up by Burl Barbee of Chattanooga, during the Sunday morning homecoming festivities at Carson Springs, Tennessee. To his right is Bishop Kelly Williams (West Virginia) and Reverend Richard Williams (Ohio), both deftly handling smaller serpents. Murl Bass, the man who was deeply bitten later on, can be seen standing between Barbee and the Bishop. The handling and services soon ended and were not begun again until the cobra was taken up that afternoon.
Photo by sister Candis Blondine Williams.

we'll do. We'll not reach in those boxes a minute too soon. We aren't doing this for publicity. God can handle the meanest rattlesnake that ever moved."

While the heavy morning grayness spread an intermittent drizzle over the worshipers, the whole hollow was aglow with excitement and zeal. Sweat poured down the faces and soaked the clothing of believers as they jumped and shouted, "Praise God! Praise Jesus!" Hands were thrust into the now open wooden boxes and a multitude of writhing

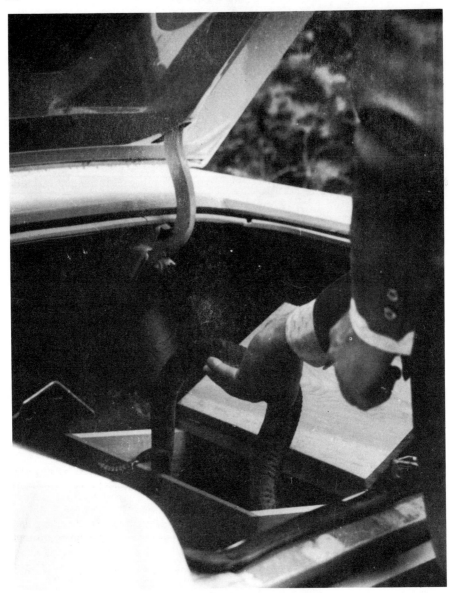

. . .the just shall live
by faith.

Galatians, 3:11

The serpents are usually brought to church in padlocked wooden boxes. Here an anointed brother opens the lid and pulls out a big one. Billy Jay Forrester, now a serpent handler, didn't realize church members handled serpents when he first joined. "I was at a store one day and they asked me, 'Do you go out at that church where they handle them snakes?' I said, 'What?' I didn't know what to say. I told them if they do, I don't know about it."
Photo by Nickey Maxey.

serpents were hastily pulled forth. Men and women excitedly surrounded the ecstatic handlers, clapped their hands in unison, and uninhibitedly sang old-time gospel songs.

Brother Danny Smith calmly took four massive rattlesnakes out of the nearby boxes. He strolled around with them in his arms, his countenance radiating with a look of unworldly peace. He held one up to his face and stared dreamily into its eyes. The snake turned its head away from Danny, swayed about, and lazily crawled out of his grip and up his extended arms. He then deftly passed all four rattlers on to Brother Al Ball. However, during a period of high gear preaching and praying, a Chattanooga brother was badly bitten on the upper outside edge of his right hand.

The band was playing loudly and the sounds from the quivering tambourines resembled the dreadful warning of an angry rattler. The resonant singing voice of Sister Eunice overshadowed the others with "They call us serpent handlers, but that's all right."

Brother Al showed no emotion. He quietly handled the serpents and then gave them up to the extended hands of another brother. Bass, with four huge rattlers in his hands, accidently dropped one. He quickly grabbed the snake right behind its tail. The snake began to struggle. It reared back and suddenly struck with a lightning movement, sinking its fangs deeply and leaving a bloody track on the man's right wrist. It was his second bite within a twenty-four hour period. He had previously been bitten in service the night before with absolutely no ill-effects. These were Murl's first bites in over three years of regularly handling serpents in various church services. The culprit was a four inch thick, six foot long western diamondback rattlesnake he and others had handled safely just a few minutes earlier.

Murl Bass, 35, forcibly shook the huge rattler loose. Its imbedded fangs ripped open his flesh as it finally fell free. Brother Danny scooped the serpent up and put it back in the box with the others. Blood flowed from the wound into his hand and dripped down onto the dirt in front of the makeshift wooden bandstand perched on the creekbank west of the church. Drops of crimson spattered Murl's white shirt just above his belt. He momentarily clutched his hand to his breast and left a red spot the size of a quarter.

Flushed with exertion, Brother Bass commenced jumping straight up and down in an apparent effort to retain the protection of the Spirit. He raised his hands and eyes to Heaven. He was inebriated with pure pleasure and joyousness. "Thank you Jesus! In Jesus name, thank the Lord! Thank you, God, thank you, God!" Murl continued his wild dancing, hand clapping, and uninhibited shouting for about three minutes before the destructive venom finally took its toll. He began to stagger blindly.

Men friends quickly came to Murl's aid and helped him walk to the edge of the churchyard. They half carried the weakened man to the hose in the little spring that flows through the dell. There the healers began their relentless supplications. They laid hands on him, alternately begging God for his recovery and demanding "victory," or his deliverance.

Brother Bass, unable to walk and in obvious pain, was finally carried from the churchyard by two male members of the congregation. They laboriously made their way down the dusty road to Pack's nearby home. There the impassioned praying continued. "In Jesus name, oh, my God, help him," came the chanting cries of the faithful within.

Bass refused to seek medical aid. Glenn Dukes, a Holiness brother from Chattanooga, said, "He hasn't seen a doctor and he doesn't plan to." Although first reports indicated he was feeling better, Bass didn't return to the church gathering. His arm was horribly enlarged and his condition was deteriorating rapidly. Several of his church brothers carried him out of Pack's house and put him in an automobile. Hours later, Murl Bass was back home in North Chattanooga.

Early Monday morning, an ambulance rushed Bass to the Erlanger Hospital where he was quickly admitted to the Intensive Care Unit. Around noon, Dr. William K. Dwyer performed surgery on Murl's badly swollen right arm in a successful attempt to save it.

Murl's hand, arm, shoulder, and head swelled to almost three times their normal size. "They had to cut my arm from the top of my right shoulder all the way down to the back of my hand." Another lengthy incision was made on the inside of his arm from under his wrist all the way back to his elbow. "Some of the skin near the top of my hand rotted away. They had to take skin from my leg and graft it. I turned black as a nigger around my stomach, up my side and around my head. They had to change my blood completely. They made a whole transfer of it."

"The decision for me to go to the hospital was strictly mine," said Brother Bass. "I held out as long as I could, but I finally decided I had to go. But, believe it or not, I was never really afraid of dying at any time. And I never did lose consciousness as some have said."

Four months later, all the swelling was gone except in Murl's hand and fingers. The skin graft covering most of the top of his right hand was smooth and shiny much as a badly burned area might look. The muscles in his hand and fingers were still quite stiff and unmanageable.

His untimely misfortune would be a harsh example to many as it was to him. And like numerous victims before him, Bass fully intends to continue taking up serpents. "I'll keep on handling snakes when the Lord moves me to, though. This incident hasn't shaken my faith one bit!"

The painful experience of Brother Bass was more of an interruption than a tragedy. As one of the faithful put it, "I'd much rather see

... be thou an example
of the believers ...
I Timothy, 4:12

Richard Williams of Hilliard, Ohio, easily handled a giant rattlesnake during the July, 1973 homecoming. Murl Bass, standing beside the amplifier, was soon after bitten on the hand by another huge ferocious rattler. Brother Bass ended up in the hospital and almost lost his entire arm. Describing his bite, Murl said, "It felt like a dog bite. You ever been bitten by a dog or somethin' like that? That's what it feels like. And he helt on and I had to pull him off. I had to reach over and yank him off."
Photo by Sister Candis Blondine Williams.

someone die in the faith than in a car accident — see what I mean?" Veteran snake handlers remained undaunted. Most of them had been through the same ordeal at least once and some more than once. It appeared to the casual observer, however, that the festivities had come to an end. It was in this interval that the reporters and television crews were politely ousted, taking with them part of the blame for Brother Murl's predicament.

"There's too much contentiousness here. Where there's confusion, there's contention," said Reverend Williams, referring to the newsmen in obvious disgust. "It's just not right for handling serpents or drinking strychnine. I can't concentrate. Every time I start to get anointed, there's a photographer or newspaper man tapping me on the shoulder. Any time you have an undisciplined group like that, you have a contentious spirit."

The fiery preacher from Hilliard, then tried unsuccessfully to revive the spirit of the occasion. He preached and pleaded, "We don't have any scripture that says a snake won't bit. It's their nature to bite. But it's still in the Bible that 'they *shall* take up serpents and not be harmed.'"

Temporarily, the frenetic pace slowed. About 12:30, everyone gathered for fried chicken, roast beef, country ham, and all the fixings for an old fashioned dinner-on-the-grounds. It was easy to feel the warmth. It was fun to see the happiness. It was thrilling to know the Spirit walked among them. They ate, They laughed. They mingled. They recounted the events of the morning. They swapped stories about miracles of healing and victory as if they were recipes or old-time mountain tales. These people are as comfortable with talk of God's miracles as most people are with gossip. It's simply a way of life.

3

An Afternoon of Cobra Handling

My sheep hear my voice, and I know
them, and they follow me.
St. John, 10:27

... what things soever ye desire
when ye pray, believe that ye receive them, and ye shall have them.
St. Mark, 11:24

As more were gathering up their paraphernalia to leave, the magic began returning to the air. Some shouted praises. There were sporadic testimonies. In the words of Bishop Kelly Williams, Switzer, West Virginia, "The spirit of the day returned and God moved on the faithful." The Spirit descended heavily upon big and gentle, twenty-two year old Clyde Ricker. He slowly made his way to the blue plastic cubicle that housed John Walls' six foot Indian cobra. On one side was a small sign, "ONE BITE WILL KILL AN ELEPHANT."

When young Ricker's intentions became clear, Walls panicked. "Don't take him out," he pleaded in a fearful, desperate voice, "don't

31

... if any man hear my voice, and open
the door, I will come in to him ...
Revelation, 3:20

Reverend Clyde Ricker of Hot Springs, North Carolina, as he slowly begins to
remove the death-dealing cobra from its cubicle. "God spoke to me through the
anointing," explains Brother Clyde. "I was told by God to take the cobra out of the
box. I wouldn't have done it unless God told me to. It's real simple. God softly
whispered His instructions to me. I felt it. I knew the serpent wouldn't harm me."
Photo by Larry Aldridge.

let him bite you!" Then he ran. His wife, near hysteria, removed her
sunglasses and wept, "Oh, God, I knew we shouldn't have brought that.
Someone is going to die." Both knew the cobra was deadly. Walls had
just tapped the front of the container and the dread inhabitant reared
its ugly head, fanned its hood, and struck viciously at the glass.

But Brother Ricker stood before the cage as if he was listening. And
indeed, he was, but not to the pleas of a frightened man. Quiet tears
flowed down his cheeks and spattered on the dust at his feet. He stood
with knitted brow and transfixed gaze, heedless to the world, ears open

... ye shall receive the
gift of the Holy Ghost.
The Acts, 2:38

"Praise the Lord," shouts Reverend Lester Ball of Greenville, South Carolina, as he lets the cobra freely move about in his hands. "I'd always wanted to take up a cobra, because we'd been told we couldn't possibly ever take one up safely. I just said, 'Lord, this is the deadliest serpent and Your name is being blessed because of this. Lord, I want the anointing to handle that cobra.' The Lord answered."
Photo by Nickey Maxey.

only to his Master. Ricker slowly slid open the glass door. He calmly reached inside and grasped the cobra's tail. He gently began to stroke its length, saying in an almost inaudible whisper, "Jesus, Jesus, Jesus, Jesus, Jesus." This dedicated child of God was receiving his divine step-by-step instructions. "Clyde, you take it out. Easily. By the tail. When you're half way, it'll be all right."

There was no music. The background was a rising, falling cacophony of exaltations.

"Praise His name!"

For ye are all children of God
by faith in Jesus Christ.
Galatians, 3:26

Brother Clyde Ricker of Hot Springs, North Carolina, at the Carson Springs, Tennessee, 1973 "Homecoming." "I got it half way out, and God said to me, in a still, soft voice, 'That's it, now take him out.' And I did." Brother Clyde was the first man ever known to handle a cobra in such fashion.
Photo by Larry Aldridge.

"My God is real!"

"Hallelujah to God!"

The deadly cobra was in his hands. It immediately went limp as if it were itself in a trance. Brother Clyde danced in ecstasy. His body jerked spasmodically, his breathing became heavy. He jumped. He shouted. He sweated. And then be began to speak in tongues—"muma-mu-mamuma-mamuma-mamuma, glory to God! Hallelujah!"

The crowd went absolutely wild. The faithful caught on fire under the spell of the moment. Someone else chanted, "Thank you, Jesus Bahbahbibah-bahbibahbah-bibibahbi-bahbibahbah!"

The Holy Ghost shall come upon thee, and the
power of the Highest shall overshadow thee.
St. Luke, 1:35

Bishop Kelly Williams, pastor of the Full Gospel Jesus Church, Micco, West
Virginia, eagerly participates in the Sunday afternoon cobra handling session.
"When Doc Walls and his wife first walked up with the cobra and we saw what they
had, right then and there I felt I could have handled it. But something killed that
first anointing. We all felt the spirit move together. We were eating and felt like
something big was going to happen. Brother Ralph Spence said, 'Come on, Brother
Kelly. I think God's going to let us take it out.' I threw my plate of food in the
creek, ran up, and got the cobra."
Photo by Larry Aldridge.

The quiet, unemotional voice of Reverend Richard L. Williams could
be continually heard pulsating through the maze of excited chatter, "In
the name of Jesus, in the name of Jesus, amen. In the name of Jesus, in
the name of Jesus, amen."

And ye became followers . . . with
joy of the Holy Ghost.
                    Thessalonians, 1:6

Reverend Richard Williams of the Full Gospel Jesus Church in Columbus, Ohio.
"We had a little too much confusion to start with because of the big crowd," said
Brother Richard right after the cobra was put back into its container. "A little too
much confusion. And God said He was not the author of confusion."
Photo by Larry Aldridge.

Ricker unbuttoned the lower part of his white shirt and collected the
cobra inside. It crawled around and lay calmly against his sweaty bare
flesh.

"Yes, Lord! Yes, Lord!"

"Oh, Jesus, my Jesus!"

"Bless His name!"

Brother Clyde pulled the cobra out again. He was at the height of his
euphoria. He almost carelessly draped the shiny black creature around
his neck and held its wicked-looking head close to his face. Ricker

And I prayed unto the
Lord my God . . .
Daniel, 9:4

Burl Barbee of Chattanooga easily handles the deadly cobra at the Carson Springs, Tennessee, 1973 "Homecoming." The power of God filled the air and eight men took up the serpent "in the name of Jesus." Mrs. John Walls, herself a professional snake handler was in a state of shock over the incident. She later said, "I don't believe it! I still don't believe it! It's unreal!"
Photo by Larry Aldridge.

stared blankly into the serpent's eyes and lightly kissed it on the mouth. *It did not bite!*

Lester Ball, age nineteen, and brother of the church's co-pastor, didn't have the anointing as he watched Clyde. He stood there praying, "Now, God, this *is* your Word, and that *is* supposed to be the deadliest of serpents. In your name, there's been a blessing for this. Lord, I *want* the anointing to take up that cobra!" Then, the anointing came—a spiritual feeling of peacefulness came down over him. Brother Ball stared at the serpent and knew he could take it up. He reached out for it . Clyde relinquished his gently undulating handful of poison as Brother Lester fell completely into the grasp of the Holy Ghost. His screams of exuberance were absorbed by the constant uproar of onlookers.

"My God! My God!"

"Bless the Lord!"

"Amen. Thank God!"

From somewhere, knee-high to the frantic mass of humanity, came the concerned voice of a solemn little spectator. "If they don't be careful, they're going to kill that snake."

"Kill the snake?" snapped a female listener as she reacted in astonishment. "Aren't you worried about the men handling the snake?"

"No," the six-year-old declared with confidence, "God'll take care of them."

As Isaiah said in chapter 11, verse 6, ". . .and a little child shall lead them."

Brother Clyde reached in the nearby screened wooden boxes and brought out more deadly serpents for the hands that held the cobra. He quickly scooped up a tangle of other poisonous snakes—rattlers, water-moccasins, and copperheads. Ball, still much under the Power, sought these too. He stood, seemingly transfixed, both hands overflowing with pounds of potential death.

The cobra made the rounds of the eight anointed handlers. Its hood spread several times. Brother Ricker lightly popped his flattened palm against the cobra's reared, swaying head. But still it *did not strike!* He slid his hand all the way up the body of the serpent, over its deadly head, and forced the hood to close.

The Williams, both Kelly and son Richard, took it. Brother Richard strolled around the churchyard. He prayed. He looked heavenward. He murmured. "Oh, my Jesus! Yes, He did, Yes, He did. Hale mi sak ti, hale mi sak ti," he said in an unknown tongue.

Burl Barbee, Chattanoogan, stretched its deadly length between his hands and lifted it skyward. "My God! This *is* a serpent! My God! This *is* a serpent!" he screamed. "This one is no meaner than the rest of them! The Lord knows!" Brother Burl later stated, "I've been in this about twenty-seven years. It's just as real today as it was the day I got in it! Yes sir, bless your heart! God bless your heart! He's a *real* God! I said He's a *real* God! Shidamikiyalalalasaylalalasaylalala. Mondalalala-melalalameahahah."

Another brother exclaimed, "He's been taking up serpents for years.

How God anointed Jesus of Nazareth
with the Holy Ghost and with power:
. . . for God was with him.
The Acts, 10:38

Reverend Floyd McCall, pastor of the Holiness Church of God in Jesus Name, Greenville, South Carolina, shouts loudly as he lets the untamed Indian Cobra slowly slither through his hands. Brother Floyd and seven more of the faithful became heavily anointed and handled copperheads, rattlesnakes, and finally the vicious cobra as activities came to a close for the afternoon. No one was bitten while defying the deadly snake. "When I took it up the second time, it felt like the angels of the Lord were standing right beside me."
Photo by Larry Aldridge.

Brother Burlin has been snake-bit a few times. But he's never gone to a doctor for the bites. We believe in God's power of healing our afflictions."

Reverend Floyd McCall of Greenville, South Carolina, walked with the cobra first in one hand, then the other. He jumped. He quivered. He yelled praises to his Maker.

His wife, sister Margie, stated, "I've never felt the Spirit of the Lord so strong over me. I was covered from head to toe when they were taking the cobra."

And it shall come to pass in that day,
that his burden shall be taken away from
off thy shoulder, and his yoke from off
thy neck, and the yoke shall be destroyed
because of the anointing.

Isaiah, 10:27

Brother Clyde Ricker of Hot Springs, North Carolina. "I was told to put the cobra around my neck when God spoke to me in a soft still voice. The cobra came up beside my face when I had it around my neck. But it never tried to bite me. So if God bids me to hang it around my neck, lay it on top of my head, or put it inside my shirt, it won't ever hurt me. I was told by the Lord to do all these things."
Photo by Larry Aldridge.

. . . they were filled with the Holy Ghost,
and they spake the word of God with boldness.
The Acts, 4:31

Brother Clyde Ricker of Hot Springs, North Carolina and Reverend Lester Ball of Greenville, South Carolina. "I just knew that serpent was subject to God," reveals Brother Lester. "I knew that I was a child of God, and therefore the cobra was subject to me — *because* I *was* a child of God. I knew this beyond doubt. When the power of God is on you, there just isn't anything can harm you. So I said, 'God, I want to take up that cobra.' And then, the anointing came."
Photo by Larry Aldridge.

Sister Margie regrets her reluctance to join the men in handling the black serpent. "There were no other sisters taking part in it, and I felt backward. So, I guess I let the devil cheat me out of it. This little voice said, 'Yeah, you do and this"ll be it.' It was the spirit of the devil

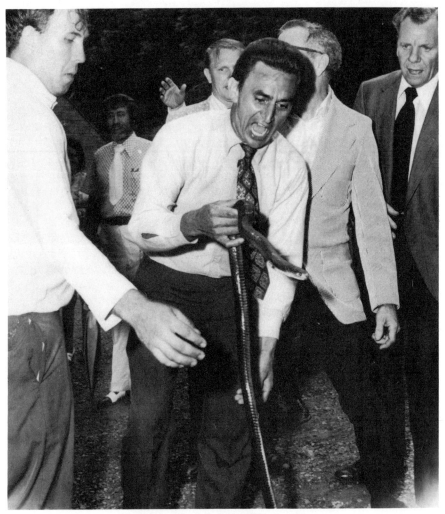

. . . and purify unto himself a peculiar
people, zealous of good works.
Titus, 2:14

"Praise the Lord — praise God," cries Brother Ralph Spence of Reynoldsburg,
Ohio, as he emotionally clutches the deadly cobra. Eight of the faithful deftly
handled the cobra in defiance of a court injunction against the little mountain
church just outside of Newport, Tennessee. The secluded churchyard came alive
with supplications to the Lord.
Photo by Larry Aldridge.

talking to me. Since there were no other sisters around, I listened to the voice that said I'd get bit. But this was the strongest I'd felt the anointing to take up serpents. I wish I'd obeyed the Lord."

Suddenly, it was Clyde's turn again. He stroked it almost lovingly, while softly crooning, "Jesus, Jesus, Jesus."

"In Thy holy name!" shouted an excited brother.

"It's the name of Jesus that does it," cried Ricker, "I *know* my God is real! I *know* my God is real!"

Ralph Spence, full blooded Indian from Reynoldsburg, Ohio, held it, jumped stiff-legged into the air, shouted, and loudly praised the Lord.

The docile snake was soon after carried back to its quarters. In it slid, noiselessly, unhurriedly. It wasn't threatened, and it wasn't threatening.

Many voices chanted in unison for about five more minutes, "Jesus, Jesus, *Jesus!* Jesus, Jesus, *Jesus!* Jesus, Jesus, *Jesus!* Jesus, Jesus, *Jesus!* Jesus, Jesus *Jesus!*"

Brother Clyde again "felt the Lord softly speak" to him. He went back a second time for the deadly cobra. He slowly reached inside the cubicle, and out it came, as meek as a kitten. The submissive reptile was totally under Clyde's God-given power. Ricker flirted with sudden death as he fondled the lethal dose of coiled poison. He casually walked around as he whispered loving words to it, held it to his face, and longingly peered into its beady eyes. He caressed it with his lips and said, "I love you, Jesus, I love you, Lord." The other seven brothers in the faith also fell under the captivating spell of the anointing. They each took turns handling it. Brother Richard Williams was last. This time *he* put the serpent safely back in its plastic container and slid the glass door tightly closed. Audible sighs of relief rippled through the crowd of observers.

This was immediately followed by a slow whispered cadence of, "Thank you Jesus, thank you Jesus, thank you Jesus,. . . ."

Someone screamed, "Praise Him! Praise Him! Praise Jesus!"

"They ought to all be dead," exclaimed an astounded Doc Walls. "There has got to be something to it—what they believe—there's just got to be something to it."

A faceless voice was loudly heard, "The man that owns him (the cobra) says there's got to be something to it! I *know* there's something to it! Glory to God! Glory to God!"

Danny Smith smiled knowingly and almost whispered, "It's the anointing of the Lord."

Ricker's calm, quiet explanation was brief. "I wasn't even there."

Another powerful declaration came from the crowd and offered, "We don't brag on ourselves; we just brag on Jesus!"

Once started, the comments came rapid fire.

"Our God's not a weakling!"

"It was just like a redworm, wasn't it?"

... I will never forget any of their works.
Amos, 8:7

Reverend Floyd McCall. Brother McCall shook all over like jelly as he took up the deadly cobra at the 1973 "Homecoming," Carson Springs, Tennessee. Reverend Richard Williams of Hilliard, Ohio, said, "If he (Floyd) was a building, he would have crumbled under the power of the anointing."
Photo by Nickey Maxey.

Be not afraid, only believe.
St. Mark, 5:36

Reverend Clyde Ricker exalts the Lord as he allows the fearsome Indian cobra to slither through this open hands.
Photo by Nickey Maxey.

And as Moses lifted up the serpent
in the wilderness, even so must the
Son of man be lifted up.
St. John, 3:14

Reverend Richard L. Williams. Hundreds of welcome visitors attended the "national convention" of serpent handlers. It was held at the Holiness Church of God in Jesus Name, Carson Springs, Tennessee, in July, 1973.
Photo by Nickey Maxey.

"Lord help the unbelievers!"

"They said we couldn't do it! God did it!"

"It's amazing to watch someone like Brother Clyde who can get anointed just anytime," stated Robert Grooms, pastor of the House of Prayer in Jesus Name, Morristown, Tennessee, himself a snake handler. "He can handle serpents when nobody else can. Nobody took that cobra out of the case, nobody handled it until after Brother Clyde got it. Brother Clyde was the first to get heavily anointed. Then it spread to the others. He brought on the anointment to the others. He was so far under the Power that others became anointed from it—it was transferred to them."

"One of the incredible things I noticed, in all this snake handling, was the nonchalant way some of these men would come up, lean over or kneel down, and unlock a box with snakes in it." These were the words of Joe Anderson, W K G N news director, a spectator present in an official capacity. "I remember one man (Clyde Ricker) opening the

Till I come, give attendance to
reading, to exhortation, to doctrine.
I Timothy, 4:13

Reverend Floyd McCall. "I got a different anointing to handle that cobra. I got anointed from head to toe. I felt like I was walking on the world. I'd never felt anything like it before. That feeling stayed on me the whole time the cobra was in my hands. This was the most powerful I'd ever been anointed to take up a serpent. I couldn't sit still. I was jumping up and down, running around — I felt light as a feather. It was a strange feeling in my bones."
Photo by Nickey Maxey.

Wherefore, by their fruits
ye shall know them.
St. Matthew, 7:20

Brother Clyde Ricker cries his loud praises to God as he holds the cobra during the exciting festivities on July 1, 1973. "When the anointing was there, the flashbulbs didn't bother me one bit," reveals Brother Clyde. "I saw them flashing but they didn't bother me even when they were popped right in my face. And it didn't stir up the cobra. If you're anointed, and you're handling, God won't let the serpents hurt you."
Photo by Nickey Maxey.

box, reaching down, and picking up three copperheads and a water-moccasin. He got all four out, and then somebody handed him a big rattlesnake. He stood there holding three copperheads, a moccasin, and a rattlesnake above his head. And then he passed them on to the guy

To him that overcometh will I grant
to sit with me in my throne . . .
Revelation, 3:21

"Thank you Jesus," murmured Reverend Richard Williams as he casually wrapped the cobra around his neck. "The anointing that came for the cobra came down all at once," confided Brother Richard. "There was no chance for fear to be there. The anointing just removed all fear off of everybody that handled it. I believe it hit everyone about the same time."
Photo by Nickey Maxey.

(Lester Ball) who had the cobra. The guy was holding this *nest* of snakes up above his head. And with all the shouting going on, it was unreal, unbelievable, that anybody could do anything like this and still be living to tell about it."

"You've got to have faith and believe in it before the Lord will anoint you, but faith ain't what done it. The anointing power of God is what done that!" explained Brother Everett Fraley of Big Stone Gap, Virginia. "You seen the brother (Clyde Ricker) that drug it out there didn't you? He was so weak under the power of the Lord that he was staggering. He had so much power of the Lord on him that he couldn't hardly stand up under it all."

"I saw it, but I don't believe it," gasped Walls. "I've never done it, and I won't ever do it!" He later added, "There's not enough money on the face of this earth to get me to do what they just did. They should have been bitten a dozen times. That cobra is after me all the time. I *know* he's vicious."

Doc's wife chimed in, "It has to be a first! If he (Ricker) had been bitten, he'd have been dead in fifteen minutes. When he put it in his shirt, I knew he'd had it. The body heat really excites them. This snake hasn't eaten in a week. He's hot as a firecracker, right now."

"They handled that cobra like it was a shoestring," said Brother Smith, who had previously taken up double handfuls of copperheads and rattlers. "It was nothing more than an old rope, a redworm, to those who were anointed."

It was this anointing Richard Williams referred to when he described the power prevailing during the incident. "Rather than God's anointing being so great on an individual, it seemed to fall on everybody at once." Brother Richard echoed the general consensus of opinion, "It was on the whole body of people that handled that cobra. The anointing of God filled the whole area."

"I'm not trying to prove nothing for me. Through the anointing and the Holy Ghost we're just confirming what Jesus said were the five signs," answered Brother Clyde in response to a question as to why he and others handled the cobra. "I want to be able to do whatever the Lord calls me for. I don't care. I'll tread on serpents. I want more power than I ever had in my life. I want to stir North Carolina! I want to stir South Carolina! I want to stir Tennessee! I want to stir the world!"

"We ought to be honest about it and give credit to these people. Many came here today to prove they were illiterate and wrong and all that sort of thing; but, I think *they* proved something to the rest of us," said Bob Davis of Etowah, Tennessee. "These people had a mission because the eyes of the whole world were on them. They had to prove God's power. So they handled that cobra. And they passed it around like it was a redworm, just like they said. A lot of people up here are going to be thinking after seeing this today."

Then, it was all over. Everyone was exhausted emotionally as well as physically. This time they really did go home. In the absence of humanity, nature took over the task of proclaiming God. The creek tumbled and gurgled down the mountainside. The breeze hurried through the treetops, leaving them rustling with the news. Except for the "ji-ji-jit, ji-ji-jit" cadence of the katydids and tree frogs, the hallowed ground was blanketed in silence. It was hard to realize that this secluded little glen had so recently been an entirely different world.

Word of these unusual people and this day quickly spread over the globe - Brazil, France, England, Germany. Some scoffed. Some questioned. But two persons who were there, who saw it, who felt it, aptly defined the purpose and expressed the result.

"They brought this here to see a sign, and God's power let them see a sign."

"I tell you one thing. I'll never doubt God again."

4

The Anointing Power of God
What It Is—How It Feels

The Spirit of the Lord God is upon
me; because the Lord hath anointed me. . .

Isaiah, 61:1

. . .their anointing shall surely
be an everlasting priesthood
throughout their generations.

Exodus, 40:15

"One night God really anointed me! I wanted the serpent around my neck. I'd seen the other sisters and Brother Williams (Kelly) have the rattlers around their necks. And so, one night I was playing the drums, and the anointing of God really moved on me." These are the words of Lida Davis, a faithful serpent handling woman from Williamson, West Virginia. "God moved me down to the front of the church, and I took

51

up a very big rattlesnake. I put it around my neck. I had just a strong feeling of love for the snake. It felt no different than if I were to have a baby kitten in my hands. There's no fear there during the anointing. Because if there was any fear, I certainly wouldn't do it. It's just a love of God."

Sister Lida does not ordinarily like serpents. When the anointing of God is not upon her to take up the serpents, she leaves them in the box. She will not even go near them. Lida gets anointments for both taking up serpents and handling fire, but she has never received an anointing for drinking strychnine. How does this lady know the difference between her anointings? "I know when God anoints me to take up the fire. And I know when He's a-moving on me to get the serpents. It's the anointing of God. It's all the same anointing. It's through the Holy Ghost that I know exactly what to do and when to do it. I am led to do it. I know exactly what the Spirit of God is bidding me to do. It wouldn't be possible to make a mistake because God tells me what I must do."

"I just feel a love. I don't feel any hate for the serpents. I don't feel any anger against the serpents. I just feel a strong, overpowering love for them. I don't want to hurt them. I feel a leading from God to take them up," softly explains pretty Sister Mary Bailey, after a church service in Micco, West Virginia. Her anointing is similar to that of Sister Lida. "The anointing of God moves on me, and I feel led to do it. I have a quiet calm anointing. He said, 'My sheep know my voice, and a stranger they'll not follow.' I know the voice of God. I know when it's leading me to go get the serpents. My hands don't get numb, and I don't feel anything special physically. I just feel the calm love of God. I feel Him calling me to go and take them up. The love of God removes all fear."

"I used to walk close to God, but confusion has got me down and out, kind of disgusted. When the anointing came on me, I could feel it come down very slowly. Down over my head with a warm feeling. I got numb from the top of my head to the bottom of my feet - completely numb," states Brother Ralph Eslinger of Chesnut Hill, Tennessee. "I had perfect love for everybody. When I got to the right step of the anointing, the Lord spoke to me. He told me what to do with the anointing and how to handle it. God gave me the anointing to do His work. My tongue gets thick, my lips feel thick and puffy. My legs draw, my hands draw. I feel a luke warmness. I feel like your legs do when they've been asleep and are waking up."

By definition, the word "anoint" means to put on, to apply, to consecrate with. The narratives of Sister Lida, Sister Mary, and Brother Ralph are neither uncommon nor typical. They are *their* anointings. Every one of these dedicated followers of the faith receives his or her anointing differently. There are often similarities in physical reactions to the "putting on" or "applying" of the Holy Ghost. The purpose, the

But ye shall receive power after that the
Holy Ghost is come upon you: and ye shall
be witnesses unto me . . . .
                                    The Acts, 1:8

Brother Marcy of Middlesboro, Kentucky, and Sister Eunice Ball of Newport, Tennessee. "I get a numbness in my hands and they sometimes tingle," explains Sister Eunice as she candidly describes how she becomes anointed to take up serpents. "I feel in my mind, I know without a doubt, that I *can* take it up and it won't hurt me. It's a warm feeling that just comes all over me."
Photo from Reverend Alfred Ball's collection.

fulfillments, and the directions, however, are uniquely individual. Some feel an irresistable, compelling force. Other are quietly spoken to. Whenever it comes, however it comes, the anointing offers each brother or sister a deeply personal oneness with God.

"The anointing sometimes comes in my hands, and other times it's just all over me. When the true anointing comes, there's no fear of the

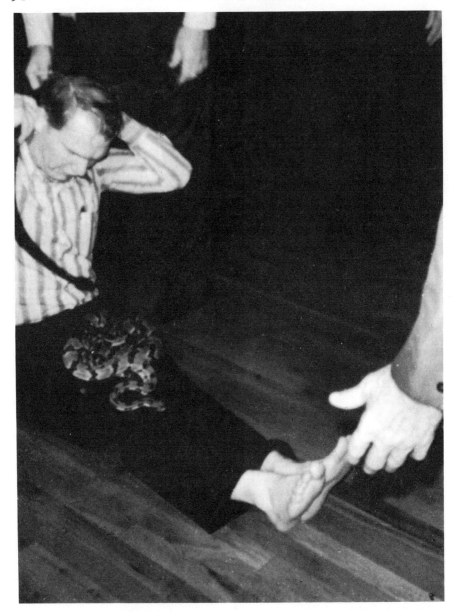

This is the work of God,
that ye believe on him
whom he hath sent.

St. John, 6:29

Reverend Richard L. Williams, "It takes the anointing of God to preach. It takes the anointing of God to heal," stressed Brother Richard. "It takes the anointing of God to drink the strychnine. The anointing is simply an outpouring of God's spirit."

Photo by Brother Willie E. Sizemore.

serpents. There's no fear of going in the box. There's no fear of taking them out of a brother's hands. There's no fear of—well, the Lord just takes away all the fear I have of them," explains Reverend Willie E. Sizemore, pastor of the Full Gospel Jesus Church in Columbus, Ohio. "Sometimes, my hands turn real numb. They feel real cool, and sometimes my whole body will feel a coolness over it. It feels something like being covered with a blanket—the anointing is something like putting a blanket over my whole body."

If Brother Willie's hands and fingers don't get numb, then his anointing simply removes the natural fear he has of snakes. He has absolutely no qualms about handling armloads of snakes when his anointing comes. This man has even taken up serpents without feeling the anointing power. "As you know, the Bible said to take 'em up, and the signs would follow those who believe. And *I am a believer!* Sometimes I have taken up serpents on faith, just on my faith in the Word, without any anointing. There's been times I've gone in the serpent box and taken them out just on faith."

"You'd be surprised at the number of people who handle serpents when they aren't anointed. There might be four or five people in the whole church get anointed to handle them. Well, there might be ten or fifteen people get up there and handle them. They're just handling those serpents off somebody else's anointing. Now, I'm not going to handle them on faith alone. The Lord's going to have to anoint me and tell me to," emphatically states Pastor Robert Grooms of the House of Prayer in Morristown, Tennessee. He vehemently disagrees with the theory of taking up serpents on faith, a common practice of serpent handlers in Ohio and West Virginia. Brother Robert is widely known as one of the best serpent handlers in East Tennessee, as are Brother Danny Smith and Brother Clyde Ricker. Yet, he refuses to take them up on faith alone. "That's why people get into trouble. If you handle serpents off other people's anointing. You can't handle them and get away with it. The true love of God's not there. It can't be. There's not perfect love in it. The Bible says that 'perfect love casteth out fear.' There ain't enough money in the world to get me to do it on faith. I'd get bit for sure. I'd be scared. If I was to touch one, I'd be frightened. But if I'm anointed with the Holy Ghost, I have no fear of nothing; I don't care what it is, I have no fear. That's what you have to have. You have to have perfect love."

"The anointing moves as fast as lightning when it comes on me. I can feel the Spirit in my hands and feet. I can feel it in my face. My entire body feels it, when the anointing comes for me to take up serpents," reveals Sister Ruth Dillon, an enthusiastic woman of the faith from West Virginia. "My face sometimes draws tight, and it feels like my hair stands straight up on end. I always know exactly what I am doing all the time the anointing is on me. I speak in tongues some, but not all the time when I'm handling serpents. Most of the time, when I am handling serpents under the anointing, I have a quiet, calm spirit, for I like to listen for the voice of God. I do know what I am doing when I take up serpents. It is a wonderful feeling. I am very happy under the anointing. And I do love serpents; I feel a great love for them."

Most people who become anointed to handle serpents feel varying degrees of tingling and/or numbness in their hands, arms, and face. The closest comparison to this sensation would be a mild electrical shock that repeatedly pulsates through them. To Brother Al Ball, this type feeling comes to him only when he is anointed to heal and to cast out devils. "When I get that way, in my hands and in my face, then I'm anointed to cast out devils instead of to take up serpents."

"If you get the anointing, you know it. It's all over you. It just goes all through you. Praise the Lord! I just, sha ma ma ma ma ma ma, oh! Praise the Lord! *Thank you Jesus!* You're just *not* afraid anymore. The fear is gone. You have no fear of the serpents. I *can't* tell you what it's

. . . Blessed be thou of the
Lord, my daughter . . .
Ruth, 3:10

"It's the Word of God and I sure do love the Word," says **Sister Ruth Dillon,** as she takes up a large rattlesnake in church at Micco, West Virginia. "**The Word** said to love our enemy, and the serpent has been man's greatest enemy since the beginning of time. Jesus said if our ways pleased the Lord, He would make our enemy be at peace with us. Praise Jesus for this!"
Photo by the authors.

He that is of God, heareth
God's words . . .
St. John, 8:47

Pastor Carl Porter conducting services at his church in Kingston, Georgia. "The anointing we get is nothing more than the power of God's. You go by what's in your mind as to what to do with the anointing. Faith is sufficient to do anything, but I like the anointing best. God put an enmity between serpents and man in the Garden of Eden. The only one who can remove this hatred is God, Himself, and I say that happens when the anointing comes."
Photo by the authors.

really like! It just thrills you all over! It is a physical feeling. It hits me on top of my head and goes all through my body," recounts Sister Thelma Whittaker, excitedly. She becomes heavily anointed and begins speaking in tongues while giving her personal account of how the Lord moves on her. "It feels just like an electrical shock, exactly like a shock all over my body. *Oh,* praise Jesus! Hallelujah! Sha ma ma ma ma! My hands get numb and they tingle. *Oh,* praise the Lord! They just get feeling real good. I don't know, they just get feeling real good. I can't explain it. Oh, Jesus! Sha ma ma ma ma ma. Hallelujah! Praise the Lord! *Oh,* glory to God! Thank you, Jesus! Shun na ma ma ma ma ma. Oh, praise your holy name Jesus! Oh, glory to God! I'll never be able to expalin how it really is. It's *so* wonderful! But I feel happy, yes, I'm truly happy. And there's a peace, a good feeling of peace in my heart."

"If they drink any deadly thing . . ." is one of the five signs found in Mark, 16:17-18. And the anointing for the drinking of strychnine or other poisons is specific.[1] It clearly differs from the anointment for taking up serpents. According to the faithful, God uses different people to perform in different signs. He anoints each individual to undertake one or more of the five signs.

Brother Clyde Ricker may become anointed to take up serpents. Reverend Floyd McCall and Sister McCall or Reverend Richard Williams may become anointed to drink strychnine. They have done so and lived. Reverend Alfred Ball may become anointed to cast out devils, while his wife, Sister Eunice, may become anointed to speak in tongues. And Brother Ben Laws may become anointed to lay hands on the sick, to heal those afflicted. But each man or woman would surely know which type anointing they had. The anointing to "take up serpents" is certainly *not* the anointing to "drink any deadly thing." And the anointing to "speak with new tongues" is certainly *not* the same anointing to "cast out devils" or "lay hands on the sick."

"Sometimes I feel a numbness in my arms and fingers, but my hands don't seem to draw up. It's mostly on the inside of me. I can feel my heart start to beat faster. That's really when I know—when I get speeded up. The longer I sit there on the bench, the faster my heart beats. If I don't obey God, I feel bad about it. When that certain feeling comes over me, that's when I move. I can tell, when my heart gets fast and my arms get numb, I'm ready," testifies Brother Billy Jay Forrester, in his usual rather shy, soft-spoken manner. Billy Jay patiently waits for a feeling of perfect love to envelop him. The fear of the serpent slowly leaves. When he reaches for the snake and gets it in his hands, Billy Jay knows it will not bite. He experiences no fear and knows he can handle the poisonous creature any way he wishes. "In the back of my mind, in the Spirit, I can tell when to pick up the serpent,

---

1. Drinking of strychnine and other deadly poisons is fully covered in Chapters six and seven.

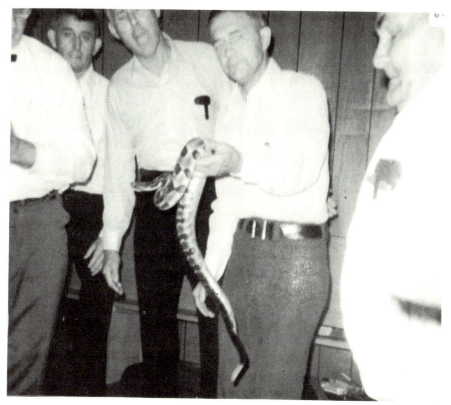

I say unto you, I have not
found so great faith . . .
St. Luke, 7:9

Brother Allen Cline handling a large rattler during services at the Full Gospel Jesus Church, Micco, West Virginia. Mr. Cline's daughter is the widow of Reverend Richard L. Williams, Hilliard, Ohio. "Regardless of how the anointing comes, it's still all through faith," explains Brother Cline. "You get the faith through that anointing to perform the signs in Mark. I have stepped out on the Word, that is, for no reason except that the Bible says to do it. I obey God, just like Moses. Moses didn't feel anything, he just heard the voice of God."
Photo by Sister Candis Blondine Williams.

or go to the serpent box. If it's already out and being handled, I know exactly who to go to in order to get it. I'll say in my mind, 'Lord, if it's really you, let so-and-so (whoever's got it) come my way.' Or I'll do a certain thing, like let the person handling the serpent reach out to me, or come near me, or something like that. Then I'll know for sure. Any doubt or fear I had will leave then. When I get ready to get rid of it, the Spirit will lead somebody to come get it from me, or I will be led to put it back in the box."

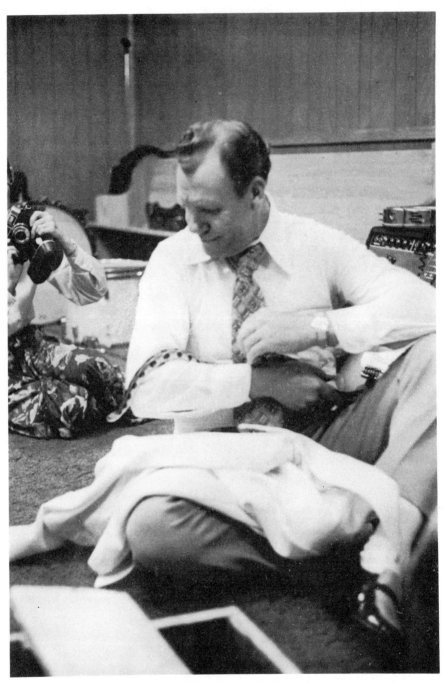

Except a man be born again, he cannot see the kingdom of God.
John, 3:3

Bishop Kelly Williams of Micco, West Virginia. In the background with her camera is co-author Karen W. Carden. Bishop Williams offers, "If I get bitten, I can't see me performing the Word of God and then turning to the arms of flesh. I can't see letting a man doctor me for something I've done for God. This body belongs to God, and God said He wouldn't put more on us than we could bear."
Photo by Robert W. Pelton.

Ye are witnesses this day . . .
Ruth, 4:9

Sister Carrie Cline handling a huge rattler during services at the Full Gospel Jesus Church, Micco, West Virginia. "We teach that *each* individual has to learn their anointing and know this anointing for themselves," says Bishop Kelly Williams, pastor of the church. "My anointing comes in various ways. I get anointed sometimes with a calm spirit. I feel a great love. This is the sweetest anointing there is. There is a motion anointing I get, too. It seems like a covering that comes in through the pores of my skin, and I can't be still."
Photo by Sister Candis Blondine Williams

"It's hard to explain the power of God," says Brother Robert Fraley, whose father pastors a church in Big Stone Gap, Virginia. He frankly discusses his particular anointing. Bob admits he has never been anointed to take up serpents. His anointment always comes to heal the sick. "It feels kind of like a chilling or tingling feeling that just runs over me. My fingertips tingle. It's strong. Sometimes it will be stronger than other times. My hands never did draw. I could feel it going out the ends of my fingertips. Coming down my arms and pouring or flowing out the ends of my fingers."

"I've never taken up serpents, but if I got anointed, I'd sure take it up. I'd have to feel in the right spirit, or else I sure wouldn't pick one up. I believe I'd know when the time was right, through the moving on me of the Holy Ghost. I don't believe the Lord would let me get bit. I believe the Lord would give me the knowledge to know if I was really anointed to take up serpents, or not to take them up," says Everett Fraley. Like his brother Bob, the specific anointing this man receives is also primarily for healing. He has no doubts about it. Everett's anointing comes down through his head. It comes on all of a sudden. The power is felt mostly in his arms and hands, but he says, "I feel light all over, about like I'm walking on air. I feel like a steady flow of electricity is going through my bones and out the ends of my hands. My palms get numb, and my hands tingle. I have even had my fingers to draw up."

"The anointing varies according to the nature of the snake. Some of them don't like to be caged up. Some of them are just like people. Some stay in an ill mood and are mean. Others aren't. So you have to have a stronger anointment to control some than you do for others," reveals Brother Murl Bass. "My anointing starts at my shoulders. Then it comes down all over my body. It's something like taking a clear plastic capsule and putting it over me. It feels like a shield. And that serpent won't bite as along as that shield is over me. I am usually scared to death of snakes. But under the anointing power of God, I lose all my fear of them. That's what we call perfect love."

Whether it is called being "anointed," "under the Power," or whatever, this phenomenon is not new. The Indians, possibly the most spiritual people since Biblical days, had frequent and intense divine contact. Black Elk, an Oglala Sioux Holy Man, had visions, made prophecies, and worked miracles. He didn't understand how, really, he just knew there was a higher power using him. Black Elk described his feelings, "then there came a strong shivering all over my body, and I knew that the power was in me. After awhile I began to feel very queer. First, my legs seemed to be full of ants. The queer feeling came up from my legs and was in my heart now."[2]

So it is that the meek and unassuming present themselves as willing vessels to be filled by the Holy Spirit. Personal relationships with God are as old as time. Age after age, spiritualists have come and gone. And age after age, they have been scorned. Still the world seems to refuse to realize that God has never chosen the rich, the intellectual, or the powerful to be the receivers of His direct communication.

---

2. John G. Neihardt, Black Elk Speaks (New York: William Morrow and Company, 1932).

5

What If the Serpent Bites?

Surely the serpent will bite without enchantment; and a babbler is
no better.
                        Ecclesiastes, 10:11

Blessed is the man whom thou chast-
enest, O Lord, and teachest him out
of thy law.
                        Psalms, 94:12

"Two years ago, I was bitten by a copperhead in Cleveland. And then about a year ago, I was bitten by a rattelsnake in Columbus. The copperhead bit me on the thumb of my left hand. The rattler bit me on the right hand, on my ring finger. There's quite a bit of pain in it. Naturally, it swells up, and the poison goes through your system. The copperhead bite hurt badly for a couple of days. I suffered for about a week with the rattler bite." Reverend Willie Sizemore is a man of the faith who well knows what it's like to be bitten while handling serpents. Brother Richard Williams was also bitten that same night in Cleveland, on the same hand.

... and whoso breaketh an hedge,
a serpent shall bite him.

Ecclesiastes, 10:8

Reverend Sam Rampley, Pastor of The Jesus Name Believers Holiness Church, Canton, Georgia. "If you've got a serpent up in your hands and you feel your faith leaving, you'd better get rid of it." tells Sam. "I have faith that my God can keep me from getting bit and dying. But, if God doesn't prevent it, it's still His Word for me to do it, anyhow."

Photo by the authors.

According to Brother Willie, the bites were simply the fulfillment of a prophetic warning. The Holy Ghost had spoken to Brother Kelly Williams about a week before the Cleveland service. It spoke through a woman who was in the Spirit, and said they'd have trouble in the city, but to take the serpents and go anyway. Willie, Richard, and Kelly had discussed the possibility of a bite in Cleveland.

Why were these men bitten? Were they not anointed? Why did God let it happen? Willie explained, "I believe the Lord looked down on us and seen that Brother Richard and I could suffer it. Because if you preach Jesus and you preach the Word of God, He said you will suffer. 1 Peter, 4:1 said, 'For as much then as Christ hath suffered for us in the flesh, arm yourselves likewise . . . for he that hath suffered in the flesh hath ceased from sin.' In other words, Jesus suffered. The disciples, the Bible bears out, were killed, tossed in jail, and Stephen was stoned to death. We know if we preach Jesus, and preach Him strong enough, that we will suffer for it."

"I wouldn't take up a serpent, if I didn't feel anointed. Some people evidently take them up on faith that the serpent won't bite them," remarks Brother Bob Fraley. "All the newspapers print that it's a demonstration of faith. But you'll find very few people around here (Tennessee and Virginia) that will take up a serpent on the faith, that way. If they do take one up on the faith that it won't bite them, they better have enough faith that if it does bite them, it won't hurt them, because if it does bite them, and they lose their faith, they could be in trouble with God. It's not testing or tempting God. It's just a sign confirming the Word of God. Up in Big Stone Gap, Virginia, the Holy Ghost spoke through a sister and told them they can't do these things in themselves. So God evidently doesn't want us taking them up on faith without His anointing us to do so."

"I think if I were ever to be bitten by a serpent, it would be for a good reason," says Sister Lida Davis. "There would be a definite reason for it to happen. Because everything—how's that scripture go?—'Everything worketh to the good of them that loveth the Lord.' And I look at it this way, too, you know. So, I think that if one would ever bite me, I would think it would be for someone's benefit, someone sitting in the church, probably an unbeliever. I believe anything that happens to any of us while we are under the anointing of God would only be for the good. If I get bitten, God has ordained it to happen, so it shouldn't be questioned. God may reveal His reason for letting the serpent bite me. I don't know, really, whether He would or not. I know God *could* reveal this to me when it happens."

"If I were to pick up a serpent and get bitten and die, I've proved that my faith is in God," declares big Floyd McCall. "I'd a whole lot rather lose my life doing something God says to do, than get out in the world and lose it to the devil. I wouldn't attempt to question God's reasons for letting me get bit and die. I'd just accept it, and keep my faith in Him until the end."

Unto you it is given to know the
mystery of the kingdom of God . . .
St. Mark, 4:11

Brother Murl Bass of Chattanooga, Tennessee during services at the Holiness Church of God in Jesus Name, Kingston, Georgia. "When you're under the anointing, you can't possibly get bitten unless God lets the serpent bite you. If it does bite you, God let it, for some special reason. Possibly, someone didn't believe the snakes had fangs or poison. Some people do get bitten out of the will of God. Then it may be punishment. There are a lot of various reasons."
Photo by the authors.

"God has ways of showing His works. There's people who say we pull the snakes' teeth and doctor the serpents up until they can't bite us. There could be someone sitting in church who doesn't believe. We would have to take a snake bite in order to prove to them that this *is* real," testifies Sister Mary Bailey. "See, they could be sitting there thinking, 'Well, those serpents have had the poison drained out of them. They have pulled their teeth, and therefore are not afraid of them.' Maybe if someone took a bite from the serpent, then this would prove to that unbeliever that it *was* God. I do believe God *could* reveal to me the reason why I was bitten. But I don't know if He would. Or maybe I would see the reason for it later on. Maybe it would cause some sinner that is sitting there, an unbeliever who doesn't believe our way, to come forward and give his life to God."

"Never to my knowledge has an outsider, or anyone outside the anointed group ever been bitten by a serpent. I've never heard of it happening anywhere that I know about," states Reverend Alfred Ball with emphasis. "But if a person in the faith does suffer a bite and die under the anointment, I believe God has used their death to help spread the Gospel. By their death, they could do more to get the Gospel spread nationwide or worldwide than they ever did in their lives. Their death could bring this about. There's always the possiblility that God, knowing the person was very sincere, a good Christian, called them out of this life because of some trial that was to come upon them in the future that would maybe overthrow them. And they would be lost. God could possibly call a person out of this life for that reason. For their own good!"

Reverend Richard Williams never expected his ever-present faith to sustain others for their serpent handling. "I tell people all the time, 'just because I hand you a serpent, doesn't mean you have to take it.' " He

But godliness with content-
ment is great gain.
I Timothy, 6:6

Bishop Iverson Pauley during services at the Full Gospel Jesus Church in Cleveland, Ohio. "I believe that if the Lord lets me get bit, it's always for a good cause," explains Pauley. "It's still the Word of God we are following. The bite is often just to let the people know the serpents are real — that they can hurt a person. A bite just doesn't really matter. It's still God's Word."
Photo by the authors.

cautioned further, "We can all get a misleading. If I offer one to somebody who feels a lot of fear, I don't want him to take it. I can turn around a whole lot easier than they can take a bite. There is wisdom in handling serpents. There are things you can do to watch over people."

The dilemma of what to do after you get bitten was faced by Lester Ball, the boyish minister from South Carolina. "As I reached into the box, God said, 'It's going to bite you.' No sooner had He said that, the serpent laid one on me—right on the finger! I closed the box back up, and the devil said, 'Yeah, what are these people going to think of you getting bit?' So I just sorta stuck my hand in my back pocket and wondered how in the world I was going to tell them about it! I said, 'Lord, I can't understand why I got bit.' He let me know it was because of people's doubt."

It is universally agreed among the brethren that there are two main reasons for being bitten "in the will of God." Since the basic concept of serpent handling is a sign to the unbeliever, some believe that most bites serve to lend added credibility to the gesture. Others feel God uses this means to painfully discipline a beloved transgressor. Unable as humans are to remain sinless, these Christians expect due punishment from their Master. The bite is a ready reminder to obey.

There is little sympathy for a victim suffering a bite "out of will of God." There are grave dangers and foolish risks in cavorting with snakes, if it is done without the guidance and power of the Holy Ghost.

John Brown, serpent handling preacher from Detroit, recalls his first thoughts concerning a rattlesnake bite he received four years ago: "When one strikes, it makes a man wonder if he's made a mistake. Did something go wrong? But we're in the flesh, we're not in a glorified body, yet. God uses us to do these things by His power. When a fear came, God took over and said, 'Everything's all right, my child.' I never had any pain at all."

"The only way I believe I'd be bitten while under the anointing would be if I'd done something that the Lord actually wanted me to suffer for," explains Brother Everett Fraley. "It might be to punish me, to chastise me. Under those conditions, I believe if the Lord wants me to suffer for something, I believe I'd go ahead and suffer for it. Whatever the Lord's reasons for allowing me to get bit under the anointing, I'd try to keep my faith and not question His reasons. I'd like to think I'd be willing to just suffer the consequences of the bite. I believe the Lord would take care of me in His own way."

"It's possible to be bitten under the anointing, especially if there are a lot of unbelievers back there in the church," says Brother Billy Jay Forrester, a man who has suffered greatly from a serious rattlesnake bite. "People may be thinking the serpents don't have teeth, or they have been milked. God could use a man in this way, let him get bitten, and prove differently to the doubters. Don't forget that God said He'd chastise the ones He loves. It could be a lesson—the suffering in the flesh."

Pastor Sizemore offers another theory as to why he feels a faithful member of the church might be bitten while handling serpents. "It's possible that the Lord has special reasons for letting one of us get bitten by a serpent. The Lord might let someone suffer from a bite to p ove to people that the serpents are just exactly as they are when ney are found and brought out of the mountains. See, a lot of people believe we do something to the serpents, something which will keep them from biting us. Some people say we take the snakes and put them in a refrigerator and get them real cold so they can't move. But we keep them in a box. And the biggest part of the time, we keep them in a house where it's warm."

Brother Ralph Spence has never suffered a serpent bite. He hopes, if and when he does, the strength of his faith will be sufficient. "I tell God, I say, 'God, I'm not asking for a bite. But if You ever ordain a bite, give me the faith to endure it.' I believe the closer I walk, the more faith I will have, and the more I can endure."

The results of a snake bite are usually severe pain and extreme swelling. Members of the faith tell bizarre stories of hands, arms, necks, and shoulders being swollen to several times the normal size. Remarks such as "His hand looked like a lump of coal." or, "His arm was about to bust," are commonplace. And, while death from a venomous attack is fairly rare, it does occur. This sobering realization does not create fear. It breeds a rigid dedication to the faith.

"My life today is in God's hands," believes Bishop Kelly Williams. "We realize God permits death. If I lose my life performing the Word of God, I'm doing it for His sake. To inherit the things God has for me, I have to go through death sometime."

6

Drinking Strychnine

and Other Poisons

> . . .he that doeth truth, cometh to
> the light, that his deeds may be made
> manifest, that they are wrought in God.
> St. John, 3:21

> And these signs shall follow them that
> believe . . . if they drink any deadly
> thing, it shall not hurt them . . .
> St. Mark, 16:17 & 18

"I was the only one the strychnine affected real bad. My wife took it, too. I became very ill for a short period of time. Then the Lord really moved for me and touched me and I recovered. Of course, I had the saints (members of the congregation) to lay hands on me." Reverend Floyd McCall and his wife Margie both both drank strychnine in the Greenville, South Carolina church. It was the first and last time this was done there. Floyd has also eaten handfuls of Drano. Serpent handling is much more popular in this area; whereas the churches in Ohio and West Virginia participate in strychnine drinking on an almost

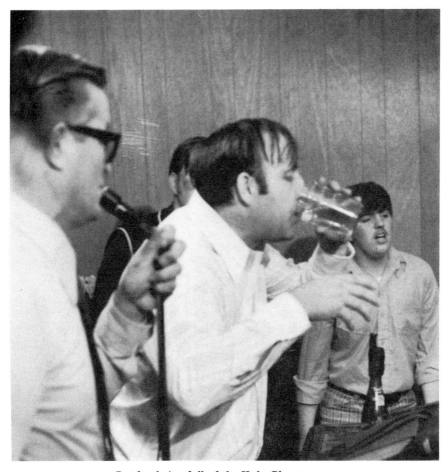

But he, being full of the Holy Ghost,
looked up steadfastly into heaven . . .
The Acts, 7:55

Brother John Holbrook of Warren, Michigan drinking a heavy dose of deadly strychnine during services. "In a revival, it's drunk just about every night," explains John. "You're up in the Spirit. You're going to church every night, and you stay up in the Spirit. You have more people, too. You have more people seeking the sign. When you're in a revival, preaching every night, praying every day and fasting, God gives you the anointing more abundantly."
Photo by the authors.

weekly basis. "I had to sit down. My feet began to go out from under me. I lost control of my body. When the strychnine began to work on me real strong, I'd jerk every once in a while. I couldn't stand sound vibrations, couldn't stand the lights. As soon as I drunk it, I wanted water. I had to go in the bathroom and get some. After prayer was made, I felt better. Most of the bad effects left me right after prayer was made for me. After the service, I came home and lay down. I could still feel it. The poison didn't affect my wife at all."

"I knew I wanted to drink it, so I fasted for it," answers Margie. "I fasted without food or drink three days before the service. I felt in my heart that it wouldn't hurt me at all. But, I don't believe I would have taken it, if I hadn't fasted."

"I felt a little tinge from it one time. But as far as hurting me, no it's never really hurt me. My jaws got a little stiff, and my joints began to be a little stiff. My speech was kind of slurred and I couldn't speak well. Brother Richard (Williams) was preaching, and I was reading from the Bible for him. I could read it, but I couldn't pronounce the words well. I felt a tightening of my muscles. It finally went away after a short while. It didn't last very long, maybe about ten minutes. This is the only time I ever had any ill effects from it." Reverend Willie E. Sizemore doesn't really know how many times he has drunk strychnine. It's been a regular practice in his Columbus, Ohio church for a number of years. This man gets a strong anointing from handling serpents, but an even greater anointing, a greater outpouring of the Spirit, when he drinks strychnine. "There was one time when we had five different kinds of poison mixed together in a bottle. It got hold of five people. They felt the effects of it, but nobody was really hurt by it. Then Brother Berry brought it out to church, on a Tuesday night, in Columbus. Me, Brother Richard Williams, and Brother Berry drunk it again. And there were no ill effects from it. None of us were hurt or even felt anything afterwards."

"I've seen serveral people drink strychnine. They have had strychnine here, often, in the church. They've had it here many different times, but I just never drank it. I've never really had any anointing for the strychnine drinking," reveals Sister Lida Davis as she discusses her experiences in the churches she regularly attends in West Virginia. "I believe if I ever had the anointing for drinking strychnine, I would know it. I would know the anointing was for drinking strychnine, just like I know when it's for handling the fire or taking up the serpents. I wouldn't be at all afraid of it. I wouldn't be afraid to drink it. Because there's no fear when I go in the serpent box. And you know there's death in there. When these hands go down into the serpent box, there's death in there. I know it. I think those serpents know if you've got fear, if you feel any fear, I really do. But I've never had any fear of the serpents when I'm under the anointing of God. It's all the same anointing, so why would I fear strychnine?"

"I've only seen it drunk twice, or known of it twice. Cecil Grindstaff of the Big Stone Gap church (Virginia) drank a glassful of it one time, maybe fifteen years ago. It never hurt him a bit," claims Brother Bob Fraley. "Best I can remember, he wasn't handling serpents. He just turned up the glass of strychnine and drank it. He's the only person I

... great is the mystery of godliness ...
I Timothy, 3:16

Sister Thelma Green of Warren, Michigan. The most strychnine drinking occurs in the churches of West Virginia, Ohio, and Michigan. They often drink the vile liquid by the quart bottles. Members are heedless of the mixture's strength, which varies with every new batch prepared. We have witnessed at least ten people drinking it before a service was over.
Photo by the authors.

know of that just drank it down with no ill effects at all. Cecil said he was anointed so strong that he didn't believe he could have stopped himself if he'd wanted to. I do know he drank down the whole glass full."

Brother Al Ball has never been anointed to drink strychnine. He's never specifically prayed and asked God to let him do it. His wife, Sister Eunice, emphatically states she certainly would drink strychnine, "If I were anointed, and if the Lord told me to."

Sister Bea Eslinger feels exactly the same way about it. But Billy Jay Forrester candidly admits he doesn't know for sure. "Maybe I would if the Lord showed me in a dream or a vision in a way I'd really know. Or maybe if the Lord spoke to me and told me He was with me. Nobody will go up and drink it just out of the blue. I'd have to be more certain than for taking up serpents. All of the signs are done under the anointing of the same Spirit. You just have to have more power and more anointing upon you to drink the deadly thing. It's all the Spirit of God."

Drinking "any deadly thing" is the second of the only two signs which are potential killers. Like the serpent bite, death by drinking poison is a tragic but exemplary way to die in the faith. Also like the serpent bite, any resulting sickness from ingesting strychnine, etc., has a special purpose. Richard Williams of Ohio, told of an especially illustrative incident:

"One week-end service, I drank the strychnine, and it got hold of me. I thought it was going to kill me. People prayed all night for me to get victory over it. I didn't know it, but there were some people in

... turn thou to thy God ... and wait
on thy God continually.

Hosea, 12:6

Sister Margie and Reverend Floyd McCall of Greenville, with Reverend Tinker of Chester, South Carolina. "This is our first time to ever drink strychnine in our church," explains Brother Floyd, a man of God who has eaten Drano by the handfuls during other services. "It looked like clouded water. The Power was really falling. There was a good anointing here to drink the poison. The strychnine made me real sick but it didn't affect my wife, Margie, in the least. We prayed and the Lord moved on me and I recovered."

Photo from Floyd McCall's collection.

Columbus, believing we were drinking plain water. Those people came to me later, crying and apologizing. They said they'd never disbelieve it again. God let me suffer through that to prove to these people that we were drinking strychnine—that we weren't playing games. I came out of that stronger in the Lord than I ever was."

Strychnine poisoning disturbs the central nervous system by its effect on the brain. Minor symptoms are slurred speech, stiffening joints, jitters, and uncontrollable jerking. Greater doses can lead to strong convulsions, nausea, and death by restricted breathing. In Brother Richard's case, he trembled violently. His overactive jaws kept him relentlessly chewing the insides of his cheeks. At one point, a sudden convulsion lifted his 200 pound bulk from the bathroom floor into the tub with one mighty snap of his muscles. The shower curtain and bar came crashing down. His wife, Candis, was much too small to get him out, so she summoned help. Family members there to pray for him lifted Richard from the bathroom wreckage and returned him to bed. At 4:00 a.m., the discomforts subsided.

Richard's father, Kelly Williams of West Virginia, has been drinking strychnine for twenty-five years. In all this time, he has been ill from it once. As Brother Kelly says, "It got into my joints. I preached thirty or forty minutes after I drank it. When I sat down, I began to feel it. I saw that it had me, and I didn't want the church to know it. Sometimes, the devil will use this to put a fear on the church. When this fear comes, it'll make it worse. If the church has faith to hold up, they can help you. If they get fear instead of faith, it's liable to hurt you.

"I felt led to go outside and walk it off, in Jesus name. I felt like if I could get outside and press that name Jesus, all by myself, I could get rid of it. I went outside and walked up and down, pressing (repeating over and over in prayer) the name Jesus, and that name released me."

In an effort to discredit what it can't disprove, science argues that either the dosages aren't enough to be dangerous, or the body develops a chemical tolerance for it. The latter idea remains a theory due to an almost total lack of research on strychnine, its properties and effects. The first proposal was answered succinctly by Richard Williams. "We don't know how strong it is when we mix it. We just put some in. And the people who drink what I mix certainly don't know how strong it is." And too, Brother Richard once lapped an unknown amount of the raw strychnine powder from his palm to satisfy a challenging doubter.

Carbon tetrachloride and battery acid have also been used to perform the sign. But, in spite of its unavailability, strychnine remains the favorite poison. And the crystal clear, innocent looking substance is no pleasure to drink. The bitterness is indescribable. When lost in the Spirit of the Lord, the partakers express no difficulty in getting a few swallows down; but most will admit to a bitterly acrid, medicinal aftertaste. More water only spreads the putrid taste over the tongue and down the throat. The teeth, lips, and gums seem to dispense the foul-tasting liquid for hours. Nevertheless, drinking poison for God is an honor.

"I want to drink strychnine, and I believe with all my heart God'll anoint me to do it." This is the wish of Lester Ball. However, he considers it wise to be sure of the anointing. "I guess I might sorta ask God, 'Is this what you really want me to do?' "

Ralph Spence feels the ability to successfully work in the signs depends upon an individual's closeness to God. "God has let me drink strychnine about fifty times. I get good anointings for drinking the poison. See, everything you lay off carnally, that's how much more power spiritually you get. Jesus said, 'Draw nigh unto me and I'll draw nigh unto you.' So, however close we draw to Him that's how close He'll draw to us."

7

Is Drinking Poisons
a Command of God?

Behold, I send you forth as sheep in
the midst of wolves; be ye therefore
wise as serpents, and harmless as doves
St. Matthew, 10:16

If I do not the works of my Father,
believe me not. But if I do, though ye
believe not me, believe the works . . .
the Father is in me, and I in him.
St. John, 10:37 & 38

"I believe Mark, 16:18 says '*If* they drink any deadly thing, it shall not hurt them,' " explains Brother Ralph Eslinger. "There's a big 'if' there. The way I see it is *if* somebody slipped me something with poison in it, I'd be all right. I wouldn't be harmed by it. I got poisoned on bologna once. I didn't go to a doctor, and I got all right. But the '*if*' in that scripture doesn't mean you should just drink poison."

"Some people will disagree with me on this," says Brother Everett Fraley. "But where it says 'if,' that doesn't sound like a command to me. If someone gets poisoned accidently, I don't believe it'd kill them. But that scripture don't mean you should just go out and get strychnine and drink it down. Mark, 16:18 doesn't say *you shall* drink any deadly thing. It clearly says *if* you do it."

"The 'if they drink any deadly thing' is *not* a commandment of God. But if you get anointed, and if God should move on you to drink poison, you are one of the people chosen by the Lord to do that. The 'if' doesn't make it necessary to carry this sign out unless there's a special purpose and a special anointing for it," offers Brother Alfred Ball. "It's not as much a commandment as the others, but there comes a time when that sign will carry more conviction to some people than taking up serpents. They would say you could take up a serpent and maybe not get bitten by it. But they see a man turn up a glass of strychnine and drink it, knowing full well it's enough to kill a bull, and it doesn't hurt him, then they're going to have to admit there was a higher power behind that. If you drink poison and it doesn't hurt you, it sure wasn't an accident that it didn't."

"There are five signs and nine spiritual gifts to be worked in the church for the edification of the church. Jesus said, 'These signs shall follow them that believe.' The Bible says the apostles were preaching with signs following them in order to confirm that His Word was true. It never did say one time that they drank any poison. You've got to really do some studying on that part of the Bible, where it says 'if they drink any deadly thing,' " explains Brother Grooms. "The word 'if' can have a lot of different meanings to it. I believe that if somebody was to come over to your house while you were gone and poison your food, I believe that God would let you live to show them people He could do it. I don't believe you should mix poison up and drink it on purpose. I just don't believe that. If that's so, why are there two people in the ground (referring to Buford Pack and Jimmy Ray Williams)? If the Lord told them to do it, I just don't see how any harm came to them. Anything the Lord tells you to do, you can do it. You needn't have fear. There's nothing going to happen to you. I just don't believe we should mix it up and drink it. That's not what Mark, 16:18 means to me."

In spite of an uncomfortable experience with strychnine, Reverend Floyd McCall defends the fourth sign. "God said if they, the believers, the same ones taking up the serpents, drink any deadly thing, it shall not hurt them. A lot of people think that 'if' means if you accidentally drink something." Brother Floyd then flatly states, "None of the signs are an accident."

Detroit's John Brown thinks he would drink poison if he were called by God to do so. "I'd want to really know it was God's anointing before I took strychnine." Brother Brown lends a different view of the questionable 'if' in the scripture passage. "I believe the 'if' means if a man wants to drink strychnine. And, if he's living like he should be, then God will shield him. Then it would be one of the signs. I believe that 'if' was put there to leave drinking poison up to the individual."

Drinking strychnine and other poisons is a rarity in Tennessee, Virginia, South Carolina, and in some churches located in other areas of the Southeast. Such practices are seldom if ever undertaken during services. Serpent handling, healing, casting out devils, and speaking in tongues are much more prevalent during services in these churches. Two young men died at the Holiness Church of God in Jesus Name in Carson Springs, Tennessee, when they drank strychnine. It was the first and last time strychnine was ever used at this particular church.

Strychnine has been drunk only once in the long and colorful history of the Holiness Church of God in Jesus Name in Greenville, South Carolina. Much difference in opinion on the interpretation of the word "if" in Mark, 16:18 is found in the Southern churches. But Jesus churches in Ohio and West Virginia, for example, drink strychnine on an almost clockwork basis — often at least twice a week during services. The interpretation of Mark, 16:18 is more widely agreed upon among pastors and members of the various congregations in that part of the country.

"Before the five signs listed in Mark, 16:17 and 18, it says "These signs,' It says 'These signs *shall* follow them,' before you get down there where it says, '*if* they drink any deadly thing.' It first says, 'These signs *shall* follow them that believe,' and then the verse goes on to specify the five signs," explains Brother Willie E. Sizemore who has safely drunk strychnine a great number of times. "All five signs are direct commands of Jesus because of the preceeding scripture, the first line of Mark, 16:17, '*These signs shall* follow them that believe.' The word 'if' makes no difference in my estimation. It's meaningless as far as I'm concerned as to whether or not the line on drinking any deadly thing is a sign. I believe it still is a sign, a command from Jesus. The scripture, in the first line of Mark, 16:17, distinctly says, '*These signs* shall follow them that believe.' That doesn't mean one or two of them or even the other four that specifically say 'they shall.' It means all five signs shall follow those who believe in the Word, in the Bible."

When people questioned Richard Williams on the confusing conjunction, he replied similarly, "People say you don't have to drink it, because it has an 'if' there. But, let's back up. Jesus already covers that before he gets down to the fourth sign. That first 'shall' refers to all five signs."

Bishop Kelly Williams eagerly goes into depth on the subject. "Jesus strictly made this point: that we *shall* do all five of these signs in His name. If I go out here in carnality and accidentally do something, I wouldn't be doing it in His name, like He says to do it. I believe if I *accidentally* do it, then I don't have the protection of His name. We have protection on "if they drink any deadly thing' because it is included in the five signs of Mark, 16.

"We read on down in the same scripture that these apostles went everywhere preaching the Word, the Lord working with them confirming their Word, with *signs following.* So, I'm made to believe that *all five* signs followed the apostles.

"God's Word said they *shall* do it. The purpose was to confirm that the apostles had the true Gospel. If I am a believer and preaching the true Gospel, the sign *will* fillow me. God *will* give the signs to the *real* ministers to confirm to the unbelievers that they have the true Word of God. We are in obedience to the Word of God. We don't try to prove ourselves, God proves us."

8

The Night Jimmy Ray and Buford
Drank Strychnine

For where two or three are gathered
together in my name, there am I in the
midst of them.

St. Matthew, 18:20

... the Holy Ghost hath made you over-
seers, to feed the church of God, which
he hath purchased with his own blood.

The Acts, 20:28

Church activities were in full swing when Jimmy Ray Williams and
his family arrived. Robert Grooms and his clan were already comfortably seated three rows back in the fast-filling house of God. The
Cramerton Mountain Gospel Boys of North Carolina were making
music for Jesus. They had arrived with about five carloads of visitors at
the invitation of Brother Clyde Ricker. The muted sounds of their
instruments could barely be recognized as they drifted through the din.
A small crowd of men were up front around the pulpit and the serpents
were out. As fast as somebody would put the snakes back in their

Events to Remember

IN THE LIFE OF OUR FAMILY

1. Rev Jimmy R Williams
   Alfred Ball
   Liston Pack
   Walter Newcomb
   Established Holiness Church
   Of God In Jesus Name
   at Newport Tennessee in the
   early spring of 1969 near
   Carson Springs Community on
   old Sevierville Road.

2. Upon death, my funeral should
   be conducted at the church, by
   the Elders of the Church, Sing
   Precious Memories and Why
   Not Tonight. Use the Cheapest
   Casket. Open the Bible to Mark
   16: 15-18. Take up the Serpents and
   drink the poison if anyone Can.
   Put my body on the hill from the
   Church, Read 11 Tim 4: 6-8
   Do everything you Can to show people
   that God's ways are right and
   Man's ways are wrong
   No Neck tie, Have the Bro's.
   that I have took up serpents with
   for Pall Barrers.   J.R.W.

The above funeral instructions were written by Reverend Jimmy Ray Williams exactly thirty days before he drank strychnine during church services and died as a result. They were written in the family Bible. Brother Jimmy seemed to know his time was drawing near and he made the necessary preparations. He had a premonition of sorts some five years earlier when God told him "he had five years to go."

Courtesy of Sister Mary Kate Williams.

screened wooden boxes, someone else would jerk them out and start handling them again. It was the best meeting Reverend Grooms had ever attended at the tiny church.

Jimmy Ray, thirty-four, strode purposefully forward and set his little vial of strychnine powder on the pulpit. Jimmy had never drunk strychnine before. He had been talking about doing it for a long time, but was unable to obtain any. He had ingested carbon tetrachloride at least twice in 1972, once in the summer and a second time on the Fall night Billy Jay Forrester was bitten by a rattlesnake.

Jimmy Ray was a natural showman — an outgoing person and entertaining preacher who laughed a lot and even injected humor during his sermons. He almost immediately joined the others in serpent handling activities. He glibly spoke in tongues, more so than he had done in the past. It sounded different from his usual intonations. Some in attendance thought this rather odd. The music was loud, but seemed almost lost in the shouting, as the snakes were passed around and around and around

Oh, my Lord!

Hallelujah to God!

Thank you, Lord, thank you Lord, thank you Lord!

Thank you, Lord, thank you Lord, thank you Lord!

Oh, my God, Hallelujah!

Jesus, oh, my Jesus!

In the name of Jesus!

Thank you, God.

Oh! How I love God!

I take it in *Jesus* name!

Glory to God!

... whosoever shall do the will of
God, the same is my brother ...
St. Mark, 3:35

"The name of Jesus Christ has caused the worst confusion of anything," stated
Brother Jimmy Ray Williams. "And we believe only in Him. The Father, the Son,
and the Holy Ghost, are only names for Jesus Christ. We don't baptize people in
Their names, but in the name of Jesus Christ alone. And because of the name Jesus
Christ, wordly friends turn against us and accuse us of being madmen."
Photo from Sister Mary Kate Williams' collection.

Many in the congregation responded with their own praises to the Lord. The excitement steadily heightened. A great number of people felt the Spirit enter, as was evident in the screams of exuberance accompanied by wild, uninhibited dancing in the pews and aisles. Handclapping and a variety of tongues added to the mood of the moment. The very air seemed charged with a flow of electrical energy. The atmosphere in and around the building was voltaic. Everyone felt the galvanic effect of the magnetic musical beat. A spiritual blanket fell over the packed house, enveloping the brothers, sisters, and most visitors. There was pure bedlam in the little church.

Jimmy Ray smoothly passed the writhing serpents on to the outstretched hands of the other brothers. He fell completely under the Power. His anointing was stronger than usual. He poured the innocent looking powder, a lot of it, into a glass of water and stirred it well. Jimmy Ray took the glass in his hand and held it up. His face was creased with the warmest smile. He looked completely at ease, content, and blissfully happy. His pearl white teeth sparkled in the brightness of the bare overhead bulbs.

Jimmy Ray spoke softly, "This is the Word." He turned the glass up and gulped down half of the deadly liquid. He set the glass back on the pulpit and grabbed more handfuls of rattlesnakes and copperheads. He sang and danced around in front of the pulpit. He prayed for the sick and shouted praises to the Lord as the serpents dangled lifelessly from both hands. Jimmy Ray showed no ill effects. There was no sign of an adverse reaction. He was fully enjoying himself in the Holy Ghost. The music seemed to get louder and the crowd reacted accordingly. They stood, jumped, and shouted. Each heightened activity extolled Jesus. They danced wildly and clapped in unison. They raised their arms to the Lord and glorified Him vociferously. The pews were packed to overflowing. The aisle could hold no more people. Even the windows of the church were filled with nameless faces peering in from outside.

"Hallelujah! I told Brother Williams tonight; I told Brother Williams tonight; I said, 'This is the biggest crowd I've seen since the night I got thrown in jail over serpent handling.'" Graying, curly-headed Burl Barbee began to preach. His first words were followed by joyous laughter from the brothers sitting and standing around him. He strutted like a peacock. His sermon was constantly punctuated with onlookers' enthusiastic words of encouragement, amens, homage to the Lord, screams, and speaking in tongues. Barbee exuberantly referred to snake handling. "They *can't* put *you* in jail for preachin' it! They *can't* put you in jail for shoutin' it! *Then why do they put you in jail for doin' it?*"

"Glory to God!"

"Hallelujah!"

"Praise the Lord!"

"How can they-I said *how can they* put you in jail for doin' it? After

... he that loseth his life
for my sake, shall find it.
St. Matthew, 10:39

"I want to say tonight that I'm not here; I didn't come to tell you I can turn water into wine. I didn't come here to tell you tonight I can take up serpents. I didn't come here to tell you I can heal the sick," preached Brother Buford Pack on March 7, exactly one month before he died. "But hallelujah — if Jesus comes and anoints me, then it'll be done. Hallelujah. Cause I believe every word of it. Every word of it's true. Every word of it's good. Because it was given by the inspiration of God."

Photo from Sister Mary Kate Williams' collection.

you get out of jail, you are still going to do it! Jesus said, He said, 'They *shall* take up serpents!' I got bit in Copperville about seven years ago. Last year I got bit at Dolly Pond." Barbee continued his rapid fire tirade as he stalked, jumped, and quivered back and forth in front of the congregation.

"My daughter came around — my daughter that's married — her husbands' here, and I seen the night he handled rattlesnakes. Praise the Lord. And she said to me, she said, 'Daddy, I believe you're all swelled up.' She said 'Daddy, what do you think about snake handlin' now?' I said, *'That's just a bite mark.* That can't hurt!' "

The throbbing music had momentarily ceased to be heard. The faithful's shouts, tears of joy, hallelujahs and boisterous laughter saturated the air. The preacher waited. Sporadic praises and sounds of tongues could be isolated above the general clamor. "When Barbee gets himself in trouble — you may get yourself in trouble — but I'm here tonight to tell you, with a heart full of love, that God don't *never* get you in trouble."

Glory to Him!

Praise the Lord!

Hallelujah!

Yeah! Yeah!

Praise God!

Amen!

"Those of us who still live close to Him won't never be hurt, if they have the anointment from God. But just a good feeling will get you hurt!"

He'll take care of you!   Oh, yes!

I love Jesus!

You won't be bit if you
live close!

In Jesus name!

Praise God!

Jesus, Jesus!

Amen!

Hallelujah to God!

"Brotherly love will take care of everything. Brotherly love will take care of everything!" Barbee interrupted himself with tongues. He slithered across the front of the church. His arms waved wildly; his finger pointed at the mass of seething humanity in the pews. Some responded in high-pitched tongues. Other simply yelled. A few women chillingly screamed. The excitement mounted. The brothers and sisters were being incited to act.

"In St. John, 5: 43, Jesus said, 'I am come in my Father's name, and yet ye receive me not: if another shall come in his own name, him ye will receive.' *I'll give you another one.* Acts, the fourth chapter and the twelfth verse, '. . . . for there is none other name under heaven given among men, whereby we must be saved.' All preachers, I want to say this with a heart full of love, Brother Pack. All preachers will go to the table in the name of unity: The Methodists, the Baptists, the Church of God, the Church of the Living God, the Church of Bible Prophecy, the Church of Jesus, the Church of Jesus Christ, the Free Holiness, and all the rest of them. They will go to the table, and when they get through passing the blessing, they'll say, 'We've asked it all *in Jesus name.*' "

There were more yells, lots of hallelujahs, and uncountable amens. Praises were again screamed to the Lord. Shouts of "In Jesus name!" shook the building. After a brief pause, Barbee began once more. He was continually interrupted by fervent believers.

"They'll lay hands on sick men. All of 'em will do it. They'll lay hands on sick men — *in Jesus name.* They'll get hold of a devil possessed person. They'll try their best to cast that devil out — *in Jesus name.* Why do they use that name? *Why - do - they - do - that?*"

And I give unto them eternal life;
and they shall never perish . . .
St. John, 10:28

"Anytime a person obeys God in the signs by taking up serpents or drinking strychnine, there is a slight possibility that maybe they will die. Maybe they will be bitten and die or maybe the poison will kill them," explains Pastor Alfred Ball. "It's accepted that some of us are more likely going to die for the Gospel's sake. However, the Lord said that if a man lay down his life for the Gospel, he'll take it up again. And we're willing, if necessary, to die for the Gospel"
Photo from Sister Mary Kate Williams' collection.

The crowd was completely carried away with it all. The little church rocked with hallelujahs and amens. Jesus was praised and praised and praised. Burl Barbee had reached his zenith, and the people loved every moment of it. Happiness poured from their hearts. Love exuded from their very pores. A feeling of bliss overwhelmed everyone. Verbal offerings came rapid fire and tumbled over one another in a futile effort to be heard above the joyous noise.

Buford Pack, 30, a former paratrooper, pushed forward and wrapped his fingers around the glass of strychnine. It was his first time to try drinking the stuff. Buford had previously ingested pure battery acid during a tent revival in Brevard, North Carolina. He was unharmed. The church grew relatively quiet. There was no music, but comments continued to pour forth from the brothers around the pulpit. He picked up the glass and calmly held the poison. He was trembling.

Brother Clyde Ricker was standing right beside Buford when he spoke, "They say this is strychnine. I don't know for sure whether or not it is. But I'm going to drink it."

"It is strychnine, Buford," responded Jimmy Ray, "It's strychnine."

Pack's hand was noticeably shaking from the devastating power of the anointing. He stood quietly for exactly ten seconds. He always had gone in for strong demonstrations of faith. This man was an extrovert and domineering in his style of preaching. He had been known to vocally disagree with a message being preached and had, at times, stormed out of the church.

The glass was raised, and Buford said clearly, *"I do this to confirm the Word of God."* His voice never raised. It was almost a monotone. It was as if the man was announcing a commonplace everyday event. The glass went to his waiting lips, and he quickly swallowed some of the remaining liquid.

"When I saw Buford drink it, I turned around to Mary Kate Williams, who was sitting behind me," reveals Sister Bea Eslinger. "I told her, 'I don't want to see this. Then I won't have to be a witness.' I felt like he was going to die. I don't know why. I was so frightened I sat there most of the time praying. I couldn't get into the spirit at all."

Whooping, yelling, praises to God, and amens poured forth from all corners of the church. Buford joined his brothers and sisters in the faith, as the hectic tempo continued as before. Brother Buford then began talking seriously to the congreagation. Some called it preaching, others simply testifying. His voice showed perfect calm and was practically drowned out by the exuberant faithful.

Buford believed one of the strong points of the Gospel was love. He was headstrong in defense of his beliefs. His first remarks were about sinners and righteous people going before God. The crowd suddenly hushed in an effort to hear Brother Buford. "He that believeth shall be saved." There was a long pause with much vocal response. "But he that believeth not will be damned.

"Jesus said, 'These signs shall follow them that believe.' " When Buford, a gifted, dynamic, energetic preacher said, "These signs," the crowd of brothers started enthusiastically repeating in unison, *"These signs,"* and the rest of his words. Brother Pack's voice remained lowkeyed and unemotional. Most of his speaking was unintelligible, as the clamor again submerged him. He continued to preach within the noise, rather than attempting to shout over it all.

"God is truth. And if you're here tonight and don't know God, what you need to do is to repent; and be baptized in the name of Jesus Christ for the remission of sins." Praise the Lords and hallelujahs interrupted his nearly hidden, but articulate words. Once more, he was muffled out. "If you don't know God, obey Him tonight and be baptized."

There was a momentary pause in his sermon. Bedlam reigned supreme. Buford was now really beginning to "get with it." He was becoming anointed to preach. He raised his voice noticeably as he continued above the pandemonium. He yelled louder – the people responded louder in turn. His ardorous ecstasy picked up the already frenetic pace. Buford was now shouting his sermon. A woman shrieked shrilly above the thunderous rumble, as Brother Pack punctuated his sentences with numerous hallelujahs.

"When I get talking about Jesus, I can't be quiet. We need to get closer to God." Buford's powerful voice was again lost in the vocal maze. Another chilling female scream pierced the cluttered atmosphere. The crowd responded to his words. His voice was still clear. "You're either in or you're out. You ain't partly living for the Lord. You gotta live for Him all the time – *every day* – and *every night* – it's not a Saturday or Sunday thing. It's seven days a week, twenty-four hours a day, and 365 days a year. Hallelujah to God!"

Buford went on for a few seconds to expound on young people. He was a man of great warmth who attracted the youth. He would often drive from his home in Marshall, North Carolina, to church in Carson Springs, with a carload of kids. Some were long-hairs, dressed in army jackets, love beads, and peace flowers.

Brother Pack continued his sermon by referring to his job. He said something about having "forty days to go." It sounded as if the youthful preacher had previously prophesied his own demise. But the background made his words totally indistinguishable at this point. Drew Click and others who were speaking in tongues particularly overshadowed everything Buford said.

The music abruptly started again with an unusually haunting version of "When the Saints Go Marching In." Brother Buford manuevered down the crowded aisle. He finally worked his way to the door. Few actually saw him leave, there was so much going on in the building. The pace of the service was absolutely amazing. Buford Pack walked outside exactly six minutes and forty seconds from the time he had said, *"I do this to confirm the Word of God,"* and drank the deadly poison.

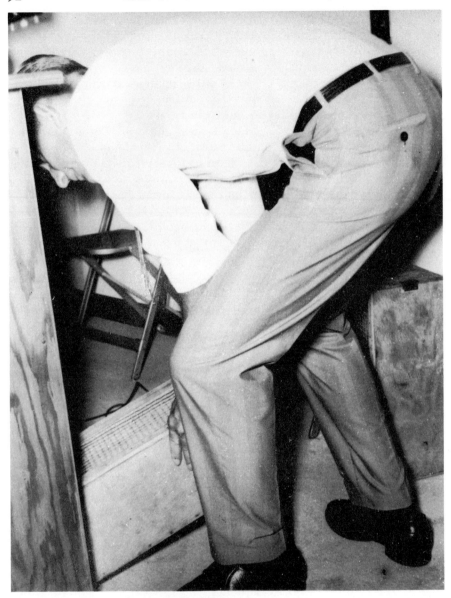

All our enemies have opened
their mouths against us.
                    Lamentations, 3:46

Reverend Jimmy Ray Williams, former pastor of the Holiness Church of God in Jesus Name, Carson Springs, Tennessee. Brother Jimmy is pulling the serpent box from behind the pulpit. This is where an assortment of rattlesnakes and copperheads are usually kept until some of the brothers or sisters become anointed and desire to handle them.
Photo by Larry Aldridge.

... perfect love casteth out fear ...
I John, 4:18

"Jimmy Ray Williams told me five years ago that God told him that he had only five more years to go," explains Brother Alfred Ball. "He said, 'I don't know if it's five years to live, or five years to preach, or five years to do what. But I know that I've just got five more years.' And within a few days of five years from that time, Brother Jimmy was dead and I was preaching his funeral."
Photo by Estle P. Muncy, M.D.

At this point, the entire church erupted in song. Handclapping, footstomping, shouting, dancing, and screaming completely inundated the melody and the words. It was better than a good old country hoedown. The whine of an electric guitar could be heard sporadically seeping through the bedlam. The gospel group kept playing the same dirge-like hypnotic medly over and over and over and over again. It seemed never ending, almost maddening.

Brother Burl Barbee now picked up the water glass from the pulpit. It was still about one-quarter filled with the deadly strychnine mixture. He slowly raised the glass to his mouth and appeared to be ready to gulp it down. Some close observers remember Burl holding it to his nose as if he were sniffing the harmless looking liquid. Barbee seemed to hesitate momentarily.

Jimmy Ray, under the power of a heavy anointing, reached out for the glass, took it, and drank it himself. The poison started taking effect soon after Jimmy drank it this second time. Before long, he appeared to simply cave in. He fell flat on his face and couldn't get back up.

Robert Grooms at first thought Jimmy Ray might have passed out "under the Power" as many people are known to do. He watched closely and noted that Brother Jimmy couldn't move. Some of the men first prayed over him and then picked Jimmy Ray up off the floor. They helped him over to the wooden bench running along the right front side of the room. They promptly sat him down and gathered around to pray and lay hands. Jimmy Ray was conscious. He kept telling those around him, "Everything will be all right."

Burl Barbee's high-pitched, strident voice cut through the shrieking and yelling. He screamed, "You don't never see nothin' like this in Chattanooga." He was answered by shouts of agreement from the congregation. "If you ain't got sense enough to believe, you ain't got sense enough not to believe."

"At first it didn't bother me," says Jimmy Ray's wife, Mary Kate. "But he seemed to get worse, and I got scared."

The electric guitars could still be heard quivering through it all. The band continued with the same song, nonstop, as if transfixed on the prevailing mood. It got more boisterous. Hallelujahs flew in all directions. Shrill screams punctuated the hubbub. It was an uproarious madhouse.

"In the name of Jesus," was repeated frequently as healing hands were laid on some of the clamoring faithful. The music seemed to palpitate in and out of the heavy air. It was low, dull, and insistent. A number of worshippers were completely overcome by the Spirit. Many prayed and shrieked in unison. Clapping hands cracked sharply. Heavy drum beats penetrated the almost solid wall of noise. Vibrating tambourines were played by some of the dancing congregation. Things became still more raucous. General hysteria swept through the church.

9

The Strychnine Deaths
in Carson Springs

And he that overcometh, and keepeth
my work unto the end, to him I give
the power over nations.
                    Revelation, 2:26

And some of them of understanding
shall fall. To try them, and to
purge, and to make them white . . .
                    Daniel, 11:35

Don Pack was quietly relaxing in his parked car near the front of the church. Buford came out the door, vigorously clapping his hands. He was shouting, *"Boy, I really feel good!"* He briskly strode up to the far right corner of the parking lot to get a drink of cold spring water flowing from the pipe. It was pitch black and drizzling. Buford turned and walked over to his pink station wagon. He was looking for a flashlight. He then went back to the spring and drank some water, "lots of it," said his brother Don. Upon quenching his thirst, Buford returned to his wagon, pulled open the door, got in, and sat down opposite the driver's seat.

Another Pack brother came hurriedly out of the church. He passed Don and hollered something about his brother dying. Don was surprised, for he didn't, at this point, know his brother had taken strychnine. He immediately went over to Buford's wagon and peered inside. Buford's first pleading words were, "Don't shake the car." The deadly poison was fast taking its toll on Buford's nervous system. Buford then casually looked up at Don and said, "I believe I'm going to be all right." There was no fear or concern in his voice. His next words were, "Just let me lie down for a little while." Don carefully opened the door of the vehicle so his brother could comfortably stretch out. The panel light on the dash flashed on. It hurt Buford's eyes. He said, "Get that light out." Before Don could help, Buford reached up himself and took out the small bulb.

People were now beginning to come out of the church to check on Buford. Some would open the car's other door. The overhead light would flash on, and Buford would cringe. A little boy took it upon himself to hold down the light button on the door frame. Finally, someone obligingly upped the hood of the wagon and detached the battery cables. This ended the problem of the horrifying lights.

Clyde Ricker left the service and walked up to the end of the parking lot. There was quite a large crowd gathered. Buford was on his back, his head by the steering wheel, his legs dangling out the passenger's side. Both doors of the vehicle were now open. Buford said, "Don't touch me. Please don't touch me! Don't even touch my feet." Brother Clyde stayed a few minutes and then returned to the church.

When Robert Grooms finally worked his way out of the crowded church, he met Brother Ralph Eslinger at the door. Ralph simply said, "Brother Buford's dying." Grooms had been a neighbor of Buford's. He knew the man well and loved him dearly. When Robert was able to get close to the station wagon, his concern grew. "He was lying in the car. They were working with him. They were rubbing his arms and legs. They had his legs up working them back and forth."

Eventually, a number of men pulled Buford from the front seat. He had gotten very still. His eyes were closed. They placed him on the hood, loudly prayed over him, and worked more on him in a futile effort to revive the now motionless body. There was a large crowd of stunned people just milling around. The heaviness of death hung in the moisture-filled air. Many were visibly upset and openly weeping. Some were fearful they would be arrested. Still, the men worked and worked and worked. They prayed and prayed and prayed.

Robert Grooms didn't join the others in prayers for deliverance. He tried, at first, but felt he wasn't getting through to God. It was as if he were talking to a brick wall. It just wasn't working for him. So Robert thought it would be better if he moved away from the group. He might be hindering the prayers of others. He finally went over to his own car, got in, sat down, and watched.

Fifteen-year-old Jackie Elsinger was there, sitting near the back of the church. When Buford and Jimmy Ray drank the poison, he became frightened and left. Jackie and his young friend, Anthony Pack, walked down the road to the bend just below Liston's house. There they helped direct the heavy traffic coming to and going from the church. After a short time, he came back to the church parking lot and saw a crowd gathered around Buford's station wagon. Brother Buford was lying on the hood. According to Jackie, Ruble Campbell's son-in-law, who was a medical student, was trying to revive Buford. Reverend Campbell preached frequently in the church and was praying desperately with the group. Buford was not breathing. Referring to the student, Jackie said, "He was hitting him in the back some way to make him breathe or something."

The men then took Buford off the hood of the wagon and laid him across the front seat. Jackie pushed through the onlookers to the open front door on the driver's side. He leaned and looked in, his left hand on the fender, his right elbow positioned on the open door top. He could see Buford's head on the seat directly below him. "I looked down and could see his face perfect. They had enough light that I could see real well. I seen him up real close on the front seat. His face was pale looking. His lips and whole face turned blue. He just turned blue. *He looked dead.*"

Meanwhile, Jimmy Ray Williams was being prayed over inside the church. Brother Glenn Wilson kept going in and out. He wet a handkerchief and laid it over Jimmy's flushed face. After a few minutes, two men helped Jimmy Ray out of the church and over to where Buford was lying. He joined Doyle Williams, Brother Glenn, and other in loud and vocal prayers to God for deliverance of his brother in the faith.

"Lord, let him recover!"

"God! Heal this man!"

"Lord Jesus -- rebuke this poison!"

"Please, God, don't let him die!"

"Jesus, Jesus, Jesus -- help this brother!"

But God did not see fit to respond to the pleas of His children. There was no sound — no movement. He had ceased to convulse. Buford was already dead.

Robert Grooms reached to touch Buford. He felt the side of his head and his hands for some small sign of life. "I kept on feeling of him. I checked closely to see if he was breathing. He wasn't. There just wasn't any life in him. He was dead!"

The church was practically emptied out by now. Sister Agnes Grooms was in a panic, as were many other women. She was screaming and crying. She ran back in the little church to get a cushion. She hastily returned to the station wagon and placed it under Buford's head in a belated effort to make him more comfortable. Sister Grooms was fast losing control. Robert felt he had to get her out of there and away from it all. He told Sister Nellie Pack to call him if anything happened to Jimmy Ray. They left for home.

Brother Robert Fraley was at church that fateful night. One of the Pack brothers told him Buford was in the station wagon "real sick." Bob wandered toward the car but didn't want to interfere. He had just been baptized in March, and it was only his third or fourth time attending this church. He felt rather uncomfortable, as he really didn't know the people well. So he stood back and let the others handle the situation.

Once more, several men took Buford out of the front seat of the station wagon. They draped his body across the hood of another nearby car. By now, it was far too late. After much more praying and laying hands, Buford's brother resignedly picked up the body and carefully placed it over his shoulder. Buford was, in the words of an observer, "limber as a dish rag. He flopped around like wet spaghetti." Liston proceeded down the road to his house, carrying his younger brother's lifeless body.

Jimmy Ray was placed in Brother Doyle's pickup truck and driven down the winding road to his house. On the way, Jimmy Ray's eyes rolled back, they "set in his head." The faithful believe he died. Doyle promptly stopped the truck. He and Mary Kate layed on hands and prayed. Jimmy suddenly came to, raised up, and said, "I believe I'm going to be all right, now." Upon arrival at Jimmy Ray's house, the truck was parked in the driveway just adjacent to the house. The doors were opened, the right one parallel to the sidewalk leading onto the patio in front of the kitchen.

Sheriff Bobby Stinson and some of his deputies came to the Williams home. They asked Jimmy if he wanted to go to the doctor or the hospital. He said, *"Definitely not. I won't go."* Jimmy was too weak to have resisted. They were threatening to take him against his will. He was strongly objecting to going. He told them plainly he *would not go.* At this point, his wife, Sister Mary Kate, stepped up to Sheriff Stinson and said, "You are *not* taking him *anywhere* he don't want to go." This was the only thing *ever* said about not taking him for medical help. The authorities were told they couldn't take Jimmy unless *he* wanted to go.

By the time Brother Clyde stopped by the house, Jimmy's mouth had become extremely dry. He wanted some water just to rinse it out, since it is generally thought to be unwise to drink water when ill from strychnine, he said he wouldn't swallow any. Someone went inside, got ice water, and gave it to him. He spit it out as he had promised. Clyde, after about thirty minutes, felt Jimmy Ray was getting better. He thought the crisis was over, so he left for his room in a downtown hotel.

Brother Alfred Ball, one of Jimmy Ray's closest friends, had been with his gospel singing group in another church. When the band returned and received word about the strychnine drinking, Al went straight to the Williams' house. He walked up to Jimmy and spoke to him. Jimmy's first words were, "Don't lay hands on me suddenly." Alfred responded with, "I'm not going to, Brother Jimmy."

Strychnine affects the central nervous system. Jimmy Ray was in an extremely jittery state. If someone touched him suddenly and he didn't expect it, he was startled. Often a serpent bite will do the same thing. Some of them seriously affect the nerves and make the person edgy. Any sudden noise is frightening. This is the reason Jimmy Ray told Alfred not to touch him suddenly. He wanted to know what was happening, so it wouldn't upset him. An unexpected touch would probably have caused him to lose control if he was on the verge of another convulsion. Jimmy knew if he lost control of his muscles, he would begin to jerk. He was sitting there praying and forcibly holding his body under control. If something got his mind off God, he would start trembling all over. As long as he sat praying and kept his mind on God, he could control himself and prevent the spasms.

All the brothers present gathered around, layed hands, and prayed with Jimmy Ray. They were begging God for his recovery. He was still in the front seat of the pickup truck. Brother Doyle Williams was in the seat next to him, with his arm around Jimmy's shoulder. Brother Danny Smith, standing in the open door of the truck, had one hand firmly on Jimmy Ray's leg, the other hand on top of his head. Brother Al Ball stood beside Danny. He had one hand on Jimmy's other leg, and one on his shoulder. As they all prayed, Jimmy seemed to improve.

Alfred Ball suddenly had a vision which he believes was a message from God. Alfred discerned by the Spirit of God that Brother Jimmy was going to die. God let him know.

Something strange happens whenever Reverend Ball prays for a sick person who is going to die. When he lays his hands on them, a peculiar thing transpires. A darkness descends about Al. This is something he discerns in his mind. It comes over him as a vision. Other people around him can't see it, but he does. The dread darkness descends all around him. It comes between Alfred and the person he's praying for. He has never known of anyone's recovering when this happens. This sign tells Alfred there's no use, the person is going to die. He'll normally say, "If you need to fix something between you and God in case you die, then do so." Alfred has had this experience four times, and all four people died.

Jimmy Ray felt, right up until the time he died, that it all was still in the Lord's hands. He believed he was going to recover. He wanted Alfred to take him some place where the authorities couldn't find him. Jimmy was afraid the sheriff was still planning to arrest him and forcibly take him to a hospital. Brother Al has several out-of-the-way places he often goes for quiet prayer. They are isolated, and not many people know about them. Al intended to take Jimmy Ray to one of these places only moments before he died. Jimmy wanted to go where they could just be alone and pray. However, Brother Al already knew there was no chance — Jimmy Ray *wasn't* going to recover.

The men continued their prayers for healing. Brother Ball was loudly asking God to spare Jimmy Ray, to give them his life. He was praying in this way because he was convinced Jimmy was doomed. At one point, Al went back in the house, away from the other praying brothers. He felt his vision might be creating a hinderance to Jimmy's chance for recovery. Was his doubt, his unbelief, blocking the prayers? Was the devil trying to deceive him? Brother Al firmly believes doubt can definitely hinder prayer. So he left the other brothers and went inside to get some water for Jimmy. He stayed for a moment, to see if they could get some deliverance without his presence.

Brother Alfred came back outside and again approached the truck. Jimmy was at the point of going into the final convulsions. Al saw then for sure, that he had been right all along. God had spoken to him in a vision. He layed hands on his dying friend.

Jimmy Ray hadn't seemed to have any severe pain throughout the night's ordeal. He talked to the brothers right up to the end. He clearly recognized everyone around him. He was aware of everything taking place up until he died. The brothers beseeched God to act. They begged God to spare Jimmy Ray.

Suddenly, Jimmy went into a terrible convulsion. The strychnine took complete control of the muscles in his body. He spoke to Brother Al. His last words were, *"Hold my legs."* Alfred didn't understand what he had said. He asked him to repeat it. It was difficult to hear because the other brothers were praying aloud. Also, Jimmy's voice was slurred and rather unintelligible. It sounded as if his tongue was numb. Jimmy did repeat his request. He was trembling all over and jerking harshly. This final convulsion was violent. Death was sudden. Within thirty seconds after repeating to Al, "Hold my legs," Jimmy Ray stopped moving. He laid back, his eyes flew open, and he was dead.

Brother Ball had the unpleasant task of breaking the sad news to Sister Mary Kate. She was in the house with the Wilsons and a few other close friends from the church. No one there believed Jimmy would actually die. They all felt he was merely sick and surely would recover. Al approached her and said simply, "Mary — he died." Mary Kate began to softly weep.

Alfred returned to the truck. It was still overcast; a slow, light drizzle continued filling the air with a heavy dampness. He told the others, "We've got to get Jimmy out of the truck before rigor mortis sets in. He'll get stiff." Liston Pack carried Jimmy's body into the house and carefully eased it onto the living room couch. Al then closed Jimmy's eyes and place his hands across his chest. Jimmy Ray, unlike Buford, looked natural at death. He seemed to just be soundly sleeping.

"When Brother Jimmy died, I just sorta walked off by myself. I looked up at God, and I said, 'God, I want to know why! I have to know why! Why did You let Brother Jimmy die?' " Lester Ball had been backsliding. He was low in the valley and had recently considered dropping out of the faith. "The Lord spoke to me in words that'll never leave my mind. He said, 'He's done his part — don't you think it's your time?' "

Brother Lester was extremely close to both of the deceased. The impact on his lifestyle was drastic and final. This man almost immediately became ordained to preach. There is absolutely no doubt in his mind as to why Buford Pack and Jimmy Ray Williams died. "I believe God was finished with these boys. They had preached all that God wanted them to preach. They had done the work God gave them to do. It was just their time to go."

10

Justice Be Damned!
The Controversy and Legal Battle

And at that time there was a great
persecution agains the church . . .
The Acts, 8:1

Fear none of those things which thou
shalt suffer. Behold, the devil shall
cast some of you into prison, that
ye may be tried . . .
Revelation, 2:10

The deaths of Buford Pack and Jimmy Ray Williams left the Holiness
Church of God in Jesus Name, Carson Springs, Tennessee, sad, lonely,
but with an unshaken faith in the correctness of their practices. The
misery of the situation was compounded when the judicial authorities
of Cocke County seized upon this opportunity to instigate legal action
against the tiny church in the wilderness. The unfortunate incident
focused unwanted attention on the area, and the serpent handlers
suddenly became an embarrassment to officials.

There is one lawgiver . . . who art
thou that judgest another?
James, 4:12

"We're going to go on taking up serpents every time we get anointed by God. Anytime God anoints us we're going to take them up," explains Reverend Alfred Ball as he and his co-pastor check the law against the Bible just before going into court. "Regardless of how many laws they pass or how many times they put us in jail or how long they keep us, we're *going* to take up serpents. It's God's word, and we feel that we have to obey the Scriptures or else we'll be lost."
Photo by Larry Aldridge.

There had been an earlier brush with the law, when Alfred Ball, several other Holiness preachers, and a sister in the faith attended a 1970 revival at the Sand Hill Church in Del Rio, Tennessee. The defendants all openly admitted having handled the poisonous serpents they had taken with them. Each was found guilty. However, in a burst of benevolence, Circuit Judge George R. Shepherd suspended punishment. He said, "We are dealing with men and women who conscientiously believe that they are right. I cannot agree with them. I cannot interpret the scripture as they do, but I still must give them credit for their honesty and sincerity." Then, in spite of a definite Tennessee state law against snake handling, the judge advised the preachers to purchase their own land and their own church, and they would be left alone to do as they please.

The credulous men of the faith took the softly smiling judge at his word. They did get their own property. And for three years they handled serpents unmolested in their church, a remote former hunting lodge hidden in a mountain valley. Then, on April 14, 1973, seven days after the strychnine deaths, District Attorney General Henry F. "Dutch" Swann decided it was time for the law to be enforced. He filed injunction proceedings in Cocke County Circuit Court demanding that snake handling and poison drinking be stopped. The hearing was scheduled for the following Saturday.

At the appointed time on April 21, 1973, the defendants arrived in the courtroom. They didn't have legal counsel; they chose to speak for themselves. Reverend Alfred Ball referred to Matthew 10:19, Mark, 13:11, Luke, 12:11-12, as well as other scriptures, when explaining why they did not hire a lawyer to assist them. This man, co-pastor of the little church, was the main spokesman. Although he did well, they were clearly at a disadvantage without professional representation. When Brother Ball was complimented on his brilliance in the courtroom, he answered, matter of factly, "That wasn't me talking. It was God."

Judge Shepherd, the white-haired, grandfatherly man who had been so tolerant three years earlier, yet who has a statewide reputation as the "the hangin' judge," granted the temporary injunction. Warning that he could padlock the church but had decided not to, he enjoined the church members from handling snakes at their worship services. Next came the first major point in a continuing series of ironies and contradictions. Poison drinking, which had brought on all the frantic law enforcing in the first place, was later specifically excluded from the injunction.

District Attorney General Swann, repeatedly referred in the injunction to strychnine as a "deadly drug." Why? To gain public support for his crusade? To influence the public conscience? And what better way than to bring the words "deadly drugs" to the forefront? To prejudice the case against the serpent handling preachers?

In reference to prohibiting the use of "strychnine and other poisonous drugs in services," he seemed to misinterpret the very law he was harshly attempting to enforce — a law which specifically has nothing to do with the ingestion of poisonous liquids. The irate prosecutor threatened, "It is time to use the police power of the State of Tennessee to stop these violations of the law." To stop what violations? What law? The existing questionable law regarding poisonous snakes, or the law the District Attorney General conjured in his mind regarding strychnine and other poisons?

Judge Shepherd recognized this important error in logic and subsequently pencilled in, on the bottom of the document, "However, any person who wishes to swallow strychnine or other poison may do so if he does not make it available to any other person."

Early in the document, it declares the purpose of the restriction is "... to prevent grave and immediate dangers..." The church members, including those who have never handled a serpent, and many visitors firmly deny ever having witnessed a grave danger at any time during a service. The church operates under self-imposed regulations concerning the deadly reptiles. They are not turned loose on the floor; they are never put on anyone or handed to anyone who does not make an obvious effort to take them. They are kept in padlocked boxes when not in use, and they are never out of these boxes when anyone approaches the alter for prayer, healing, contributing an offering, or for any other reason.

The receivers of the injunction disagreed with several of its statements. It accused them of "... jeopardizing the peace, good order and morals of society." They are quick to recall that their former ways of life, before conversion and introduction into the faith, were a much greater threat to the peace, good order, and morals of society than anything they have done since. "They ought to thank the Lord people like us got right with God," Brother Al suggests.

They are particularly disheartened by the phrase in Section III: "... it being one of the rituals of the church to test the faith and sincerity of belief of the church members." This is the most universally misunderstood aspect of their religion. Handling serpents is not, they emphasize, a *test* of faith. It is to confirm the veracity of the Bible to others. Mark, 16:17-18 *says* it can be done; they *show* it can be done.

A similar charge that "... strychnine was placed on the altar in the pulpit and members were asked to come forward and test their faith by drinking said strychnine..." is declared an outright lie. The participants insistently repeat that no one is *ever* asked or encouraged by another to take part in these rituals.

The injunction referred to the strychnine deaths as "human sacrifice," and said "... the faithful would not permit..." medical attention for Reverend Jimmy Ray Williams. Brother Ball answered, "In order to offer a human sacrifice, you would be deliberately killing someone. These men had no idea that they would die." Brother Jimmy's response to frequent suggestions that he allow medical aid was, "God will take care of me."

Subsequently, family members and church leaders were able to persuade the county coroner to change the death ruling from suicide to accidental. As Reverend Ball, a close friend to both victims, assured, "They *did not* believe they would die. They did not believe they would be hurt. They were anointed to do this and told to only by God. They didn't have any plans of dying."

The court order was served and accepted. For several nights there were state and local officials in attendance at the church services. Snakes were present but not handled. The policing of the primitive worshipers steadily lost importance, and, as before, there was a respite from lawmen, newsmen, and wearisome misinformation.

On Sunday, July 1, 1973, the Holiness serpent handlers exploded into the headlines all over the world. Their Homecoming, alias National Convention, created a new tidal wave of attention that bruisingly swept away the tranquility of the past few months.

The lively serpent handling activities were in direct violation of the injunction. The members had asserted, throughout the legal procedures, that they would not and could not be stopped from handling their snakes, if and when God so moved them. Once more, this demonstration thrust them headlong into the battle of allegiance to God or compliance with the law of man. This time the charges were more serious. Conviction of contempt of court could result in a fine, a jail term, or both. Again, on Saturday, July 28, 1973, Holiness preachers, placing their faith in God, sat in front of an exasperated court.

The neat brick building that housed the Cocke County Court, county offices, and jail was situated between the town's main street and the railroad tracks. Its lawn was well trimmed, and, in Newport, as in most rural county seats, the courthouse or the courtyard is the place to be on Saturday morning.

There was an assortment of vegetables for sale under a shade tree. All the benches were full of bristly old-timers, each with one cheek stretched over a golf ball size wad of tobacco. Some of the farmers and country folk had shaved and cleaned up; most hadn't bothered. The majority wore a white shirt under their overalls—after all, it was Saturday.

The venerable courtroom was aging gracefully. Its thickly plastered walls were painted the familiar academic green. The heavy wooden benches were darkened by years of occupancy. The judge's bench, the jury box, and the tables for other court officials were separated from the spectators by an ancient wood rail with a creaky swinging gate. The giant leather judge's chair looked natural for its purpose, if a little out of place in the general decor. The witness stand was a green upholstered office chair.

There was no air conditioning, so the oversized windows were open, allowing boisterous street noises to mingle with the quiet, solemn atmosphere inside. Huge trucks, heading to or from the nearby canning factories, were often the dominant sound as they ground through numerous gears or sighed a reluctant surrender to air brakes.

The publicity resulted in a packed courtroom. The small talk dwindled when the youthful sheriff, Bobby Stinson, interrupted with his "all rise" chant, reciting the call to order in this-is-a-recording style. Judge Shepherd settled himself, thumbed through the giant docket, and rather resignedly began. His soft-spoken manner belied his sternness.

The opening remarks by District Attorney General Swann again brought to the public ear the drinking of strychnine and the deaths in April, both irrelevant to this case and legal according to Judge Shepherd's comment in the April injunction.

As he continued, the prosecutor's predominant irritation over the case and his motivation for pressing it came to the fore. Mr. Swann clearly revealed his hand when he pleaded, "If snake handling is *not* stopped at this fundamentalist church, Cocke County, Tennessee, will become the snake handling capitol of the world!" The idea of this church growing in popularity and becoming a predominant one in Cocke County was anathema to him, and resulted in his intolerance of its differences.

The defendants, whose religious convictions do not allow them to swear, "affirmed" that what they said would be the truth. Neither Alfred Ball or his copastor of the church, denied taking up serpents. Several witnesses testified as having seen them do so, and the preachers calmly accepted this. "We don't want anybody to lie."

Reverend Jake Knight, pastor of a nearby Church of God, testified under the Attorney General's questioning that he had seen several of the brothers, including Alfred Ball, handle the cobra at the Homecoming. Alfred, again their spokesman, cross-examined:

"Did you say that you saw *me* handling the cobra?"

"Well, there were several people there," answered the minister.

"But didn't you just *say* you saw *me* handling it?"

"Yes, I did."

"Did you, in fact, see me handling the cobra?"

"I can't be sure," the witness hedged.

"Your Honor," Ball stated, "I wasn't even on the church grounds when the cobra was handled. I didn't even see it handled, much less take it up, myself."

The ensuing courtroom conversations ranged from informal to lackadaisical. The prosecutor kept a running harangue about the recent strychnine deaths and the Homecoming bite victim. A few caustic comments were made and a few judgments were passed.

Judge Shepherd presumptiously suggested that the scriptural passage the Holiness members base snake-handling on should not even be in the Bible. He said, in a typically unjudicial statement of logic, "There is such a small percentage of people who believe in this, they must be wrong." At one point, however, he did admit, "I believe these men honestly believe they are obeying their religion. . ." Swann then volunteered his scholarly view that revised versions of the Bible did not contain the verses in question regarding serpent handling. However, he could not prove this statement to be correct, nor could anyone else, for revised versions of the *Bible do* include these verses.

Finally, the judge sentenced both preachers to ten days in jail and a fifty dollar fine. Whereupon the Attorney General bolted from his chair, loudly protesting and wildly waving his arms.

"But, your Honor, I had requested the maximum penalties!"

"Oh," replied Judge Shepherd, surprised, unruffled, but obviously puzzled. He scratched his head dubiously. Then came his stunning question—a shocker! "What is the maximum?"

The courtroom buzzed with questioning disbelief as he pulled a massive law book over to look up the penalty for contempt of court. The good judge discovered the maximum was ten days in jail and fifty dollars fine *for each count*. Having previously established the number of proven times each preacher had violated the injunction, he amended the sentences to twenty days and $100 (two counts for Alfred Ball) and thirty days and $150 (three counts for Liston Pack). Satisfied, Attorney General Swann quietly took his seat, leaned back, and smiled.

The judge allowed thirty days for the preachers to pay the fines and offered to lend them the money if they couldn't get it. Then, he conditionally suspended the jail sentences. "I'm going to do you boys the way I do the drunks. We leave them alone 'til they take a drink. We'll leave you alone 'til you pick up a snake."

On Friday, August 10, 1973, Richard Strehlow, the Tennessee state chairman of the American Civil Liberties Union announced the organization had voluntarily undertaken the snake handling issue. Believing that the First Amendment guarantee of freedom of religious practice was being violated, skillful young ACLU lawyers E. Michael Ellis and Jim Emison began laying groundwork for moving the case toward the United States Supreme Court. Since the legal action would be taken against an existing law rather than a person, the acquisition of lawyers was more acceptable to the preachers.

Eight days later, on Saturday, August 18, Reverend Alfred Ball was attending the funeral of a church member's father. The dapper Cocke County sheriff and a deputy patiently waited in their patrol car parked outside the Carson Springs Church of God. Bobby calmly puffed away on a slim, fresh cigar. They had been ordered to pick up and jail Brother Al on sight.

By this time, a mutual respect had developed between Sheriff Stinson and the harried preachers. Stinson found this task particularly distasteful, but he was left no choice. The judge had issued an arrest order that morning. He had notified Pack, but was unable to contact Reverend Ball.

The arrest of the two had been ordered for a further violation of the injunction, when they again handled snakes at church. This was witnessed August 4, by Tennessee Bureau of Investigation agent, Ed Ashburn. The second reason given for picking them up was failure to pay their fines. However, investigation revealed two inconsistencies in the arrest order— 1) only twenty-one of the thirty days allotted by the court for paying the fines had elapsed; 2) the judge had instructed them at the last hearing to prepare to come to jail the morning after they

Is the law against the
promises of God?
Galatians, 3:21

Mike Ellis and Jim Emeson, American Civil Liberties Union attorneys, in conference with Brother Pack and Brother Ball. This meeting took place just outside the courtroom in Newport, Tennessee. "I don't care if you tell them (the court) that I take up serpents," preached Reverend Ball to his congregation the night before his trial. "I don't want you to ever lie about it. I just want you to tell the truth. I take up every serpent God tells me to take up. I don't intend to quit. There's no backing up room!"
Photo by Larry Aldridge.

took up the next serpent, and that particular serpent handling incident occurred two full weeks before the arrest order was given.

According to the order, both men were to turn themselves in after church services that Saturday night. In the meantime, the authorities received a malicious "tip" that Alfred was planning to run—to leave town. This was done by someone extremely close to Brother Al—one he'd never suspect of such an act. Promptly, a warrant was sworn out for Al's immediate arrest. Sheriff Stinson found stalking a preacher at a funeral was not a pleasant task.

When the funeral was over, Reverend Ball briskly walked out of the church and pointedly approached the cigar-smoking sheriff and his deputy. Bobby Stinson hastily apologized for the intrusion and explained the circumstances.

"Why, you know me better than that," Alfred smiled. "You know I'd never do anything like that."

Much relieved and in full agreement with the sincere young preacher, Sheriff Stinson read him the warrant. He then instructed Brother Al, as he had Pack, to be at the courthouse to turn himself in at 9:30 that night. Sister Eunice, Alfred's wife, smiled through her tears as she warmly joked with the accommodating sheriff, "Get that cigar out of your mouth, Bobby, we're Holiness people." Duly chastised, the wiry lawman flashed his boyish grin, hid his stogie, eased into his cruiser, and drove away.

The service in the hollow that night was typical—no more and no less emotional than usual. There were a few comments made among members and from the pulpit about going to jail, but no one dwelled on it. At 9:15, the preachers exited from the church and piled into Brother Danny Smith's old blue automobile. The speedometer didn't work and the car shook and rattled as Brother Liston, obviously excited, laid his foot heavily on the gas pedal. The vehicle lurched and groaned as it sped down the treacherously snaking mountain dirt road. Pack was whistling and singing, Ball was holding on and praying as they flew down the city streets and through stop signs at breakneck speeds.

They finally arrived at the courthouse. It was 9:28. The sheriff was not there, so the prisoners waited restlessly in the hallway. Light banter passed between the preachers and the deputies on duty. Church members began drifting in and a few reporters appeared. Had it been agreeable to the authorities, over fifty church members had pledged to serve jail time in place of their pastors.

When Stinson subsequently arrived, everyone milled around and chatted amiably for awhile. He then escorted the men up to the cell level, and secured them in the jail's hospital room. It was exactly 10:05. Brother Ball immediately sat down and wrote the first words in his prison diary: "In jail again! For the Word of God and the testimony of Jesus Christ."

"We'll take good care of them," Sheriff Stinson told the friendly group of well-wishers waiting downstairs. "Tell the folks these boys aren't going to be mistreated. I'll see to that!"

At 11:04, Pastor Ball's dry humor broke through the otherwise humorless circumstances. He wrote: "A praying mantis just flew in the window. There are now two Holiness preachers and a praying mantis bug in this jail cell." He later wrote of the mantis, "He's sitting up on the wall just kinda looking at me. As if he were really praying. Well, who knows? Maybe he is."

The preachers had all they needed, including Sunday dinner the next day from their families. Reverend Ball was mildly disappointed in his

Yea, and all that will live godly in
Christ Jesus shall suffer persecution.
2, Timothy, 3:12

Reverend Alfred Ball and his co-pastor being escorted to their cell by Sheriff Bobby Stinson. "Jail won't last forever, God will," said Brother Ball with his usual quiet sincerity. "I'm going to continue to preach it like it really is, because we're going to pay for it anyway. I've been in jail four times over the word of God, but I've never shed a drop of blood over it. Are you willing? I hope I am."
Photo by Larry Aldridge.

unjail-like quarters. He had planned to use the sentence time to "witness" to other prisoners. But, aside from a nasty cold caught by both pastors, they were reasonably comfortable. On Wednesday, August 22, their fines were paid. Alfred's $100 was taken care of by his mother-in-law. Brother Richard Williams of Columbus, Ohio, sent $150 to cover his co-pastor's. The preachers were free at last.

There was a perfunctory hearing held the following Saturday. Both sides conferred briefly and agreed to move the case up to September 27.

On that Thursday morning, the professionalism of the ACLU lawyers was a stark contrast to the previous inept courtroom procedures. The comments and activities now became reminiscent of a scene from Perry Mason. Judge Shepherd was conscientiously careful in his choice of words and extremely guarded in his statements and conclusions. It was certainly a welcome change. The man was obviously uncomfortable with the situation. Shepherd was now interested only in getting the controversial case off his hands and out of his courtroom.

Most of the hearing was devoted to legal tactics by the ACLU. They were trying to smooth out the record so the case could be appealed. The young attorneys easily went through all the required formal technicalities. Neither side was allowed to call witnesses, although the prosecution and defense did stipulate what the testimonies would have been. All agreed to having the injunction made permanent, and Judge Shepherd ruled that the jail terms must be served. These decisions enabled ACLU defense attorneys to appeal both the injunction and the contempt of court fines and sentences. The first major battle had been won.

Judge Shepherd tried to extract a promise from Reverends Ball and Pack that they would not handle snakes while the case was being appealed. He said, "They're not going to Heaven or Hell because they do or don't handle snakes."

Neither preacher could, in good conscience, agree to this. ACLU attorney Ellis responded with, "When they are called upon to handle serpents, it is not voluntary, it is the Holy Spirit using them to confirm the Word of God to the non-believers." The only insurance offered was that the men would not handle snakes unless "anointed by the Holy Spirit" to do so.

"What do you mean by "ANNOINT?" Judge Shepherd demanded. "Somebody bring me a dictionary!"

The book was produced, and he began leafing through its pages. After a long pause, Shepherd said in a voice tinged with impatience and sarcasm, "That *word* isn't even in the dictionary."

Henry Swann smugly smiled, seemingly in agreement with the judge's revelation. Another court official took the dictionary and opened it. Reverend Ball offered in a low but audible tone, "It only has one 'n,' your Honor." The word was found and its definition read to the court.

Until higher courts hear the appeal, it is all over. The judge was anxious to unload the case. But his and the prosecutor's overriding preoccupation with the county's reputation will never be understood by Newport's decent townspeople or anyone in the general vicinity. Cocke County has been infamous for many years for its acceptable corruption and a not so open-hearted citizenry. In the words of a long-time resident of a nearby community, "There's hardly a week passes that somebody isn't killed in Cocke County. Moonshine running makes it dangerous. The people will do anything in the world for you, if they like you. If they don't like you, you might accidentally not live."

There is another thriving business in the area that is intolerant to its becoming the "snake handling capitol of the world." A native East Tennesseean once remarked, "If you could put a tent over the whole city of Newport, you'd have the largest whorehouse in the country."

All confrontations were almost friendly. Not once have the church people most directly involved become angry, resentful, or bitter. They are convinced all their trials, imprisonments, and discomforts have been for the good of the Gospel. The Bible speaks of jailing and persecution, and they are willing to sustain it for their Lord. The prevailing Christian attitude was visible when a houseful of "amens" ended a prayer by Reverend Ball in one of his services, "We pray also for Judge Shepherd. We figure he has been as fair with us as he could be, but we are not changed in our faith."

11

Obey God's Law or Man's Law?

But I will deliver thee in that day,
saith the Lord . . .
                    Jeremiah, 39:17

Concerning zeal, persecuting the
church; touching the righteousness
which is in the law, blameless.
                    Philippians, 3:6

"The laws don't stop us from taking up serpents," explains Reverend
Floyd McCall. "When we get the anointing from God, we take them up
no matter where we are. We believe in the law, but God's law was made
before man's law. And we believe in obeying God's law. We used to
hold quite a few street meetings and handle serpents right on the main
street of different towns, a few years ago. We always tried to get
permission from the authorities, but if they refused to cooperate, and
God anointed us, we'd handle the serpents anyway. We never seemed to
run into any trouble with the law in those days. But that's all changed
now."

"I would prefer to be able to obey the state law and all the laws. I
believe we should obey the law. However, when the law of the state or

114

the Federal Government, whichever the case may be, becomes contrary to God's law or what God says to do, then I take God's law." Brother Alfred Ball strongly feels the law in Tennessee against serpent handling is unfair. It is wrong. He intends to fight it — to do everything in this power to get it taken off the books, or at least revised. Alfred believes that the salvation of his soul doesn't depend on obeying a man-made law. But he believes it does depend on his obeying God's law. "If I choose to be a saved man — and I do — I don't have any choice. I have every intention of enduring until the end and being saved in the end. If I obey a state law that says I can't obey God, then I have made a man my God. I have said that I depend more upon that man than I do God. In other words, I fear the man worse than I do God. Jesus said to not fear man who only destroy the body, but fear God who could destroy both body and soul. If it was baptizing, if it was praying, or whatever it was, and the state law said it was something I couldn't do, and God said I had to do it, then I would choose God's law."

"They don't give you any choice. If you're not endangering anybody else's life, they say 'Well, you can't say you're not endangering *anybody's* life — you're endangering your own life.' In Virginia, they fine people for endangering their *own* life." This is the view given by Brother Everett Fraley of Big Stone Gap, Virginia, who has closely observed the legal machinery in action there. "I'd hate to walk into a church house and take a man who was under the anointing of God by the hand and lead him out and put him in jail. I'd be afraid to do that myself. I'd be afraid the Lord would strike me down right there. But these people don't know the power of the Lord, and they don't fear God. According to the Bible, you should fear God. I don't believe the law should interfere with what's in the scriptures."

What would Sister Lida Davis do if there were a law in West Virginia against serpent handling during religious services? Would she break the law? "I'd still take them up. It's always better to obey God's Word, His law, than to obey something man says you have to do. Yes, I would keep on doing it even if they put me in jail. Like my husband asked me, 'Supposin' you go over to church and take up serpents, and they call me to come get you out of jail?' I says to him, 'No, don't come get me. I'll just stay in jail with the rest of them.' I'm not out to save my hide. I'm not afraid of being in jail over the Word of God."

"We're in the city limits, and we still handle serpents," says Pastor Willie E. Sizemore. He is referring to the fact that the city of Columbus, Ohio, has an ordinance banning serpent handling activities in churches. "We feel we are supposed to serve God and not man. When it comes to a conflict between the law of God and the law of man, well, it's simple. We have no choice but to obey the law of God. We obey the law of the land only so long as it is pleasing to God. We find that the apostles, at one time, were forbidden to do the things they were doing. The apostles were being persecuted in an attempt to get them to stop what

Shall not Shimei be put to death
for this, because he cursed the
Lord's anointed?
2 Samuel, 19:21

Brother Glenn Dukes of Chattanooga, Tennessee, takes serpents up in The Holiness Church of God in Jesus Name, Kingston, Georgia. "We are really between two powers," explains Brother Glenn in reference to obeying God's law or man's. "It's no easy task. But, when you make up your mind to turn from the power of the devil, God will give you the strength for anything."
Photo by the authors.

For it is sanctified by the
word of God, and prayer.
Timothy, 4:5

Brother Croy, son of Pastor Charles Croy of the Apostolic Church in Warren, Michigan. "They can tear Mark, 16 out of the Bible, but it wouldn't do any good," exclaims Brother Croy. "The truth is burned into my heart. I know that serpent handling is right!"
Photo by the authors.

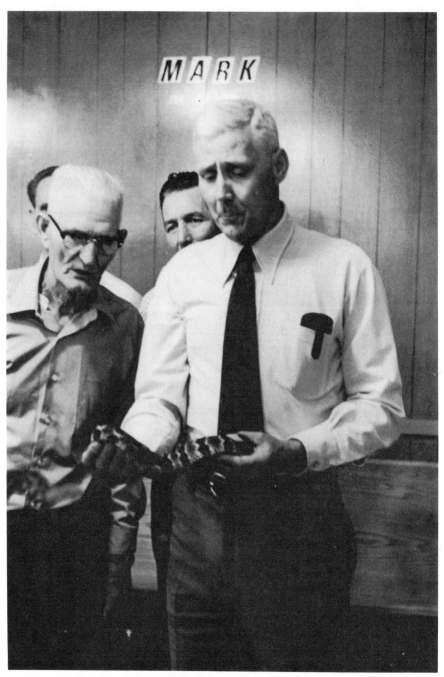

And we are his witnesses of these
things; and so is also the Holy
Ghost, who God hath given to
them that obey him.

The Acts, 5:32

Brother Dave Sexton of the Full Gospel Jesus Church in Micco, West Virginia.
"Some people say, 'Dave, why do you take up serpents?' Because God told me to.
Because I'm a believer of the Gospel. God said if I believed the Gospel, I could take
them up."
Photo by the authors.

Be glad then . . . and rejoice
in the Lord your God . . .
Joel, 2:23

Reverend O. V. Shoupe of Monterey, Tennessee. Note the serpent boxes. Reverend Shoupe has been handling serpents longer than any living man. He was brought into the faith in the early 1900's. "Once you've received a serpent bite, if you've got the faith right then and there to endure that bite, you can go through it. If you don't have the faith, or when one bites you and you get scared, if you don't believe you can stand it, you might as well go to the doctor then."
Photo by the authors.

they were doing. They were performing signs, miracles and wonders. Signs, miracles, and wonders were being done in the name of the Holy Child, Jesus. In response to the persecution, Peter and the apostles say in the Word of God, 'We ought to obey God rather than men.' You can see this for yourself. Just look in Acts, 5:29. That's just about as clear as it can be."

"When the laws of man interfere with the laws of God, I have to obey the laws of God. It is better to obey God," explained Reverend Richard Williams. "When it comes to making a decision between obeying the laws of man and the laws of God, I have to obey the laws of God. I have no real choice. I feel it's always better to simply obey the Lord."

"Naturally, nobody wants to go to jail for this. But if I get anointed, I'm going to take up serpents. No matter what! If the law officers are standing right there watching me, and I get anointed, I'm still going to take up serpents. Whatever is the Lord's will." Billy Jay Forrester doesn't believe there should be a law against the practice of serpent handling in the churches. He acknowledges the fact that it really doesn't make any difference to members whether or not there is a law against it. They will do it anyway, simply because it is in the Bible. And he sincerely believes the words in the Bible take precedence over any of man's laws. "In olden times, many people were killed over the Word. John the Baptist was beheaded for what he believed. Jesus said we'd be persecuted and brought before council for his name's sake. I believe He'll take care of us when trouble comes. I *would* disobey the laws of the land in order to obey God's laws. We have to obey God's law in order to enter into the Kingdom of Heaven."

"I don't think they had a right under the Constitution of the United States to pass a law that would go against the freedom of religion," protests Brother Robert Fraley. "I can see the law saying you couldn't handle serpents to endanger any *other* person, other than yourself. If I handle a serpent under the anointing of the Holy Ghost, I don't feel I'm endangering myself. If they feel I might endanger another person, I believe the law would be all right. If I was handling serpents in a group, somebody else would either have to come up and take the serpent from me, out of my hands, or I would put it back in the box and let them take it out themselves. I have seen it done both ways. I wouldn't offer it to anyone."

"Oh, Glory to God, I'd take them up even if there was a law against it in West Virginia. We'd all be willing to go to jail," says Sister Thelma Whittaker. "Yes I'd violate the law, because I'd be obeying God's Word which is much more important. It's the Word. God's Word says we *can* and *should* do it. So, it is not of the devil and wrong. If it's in the Scripture, then we do whatever He tells us we must do. That's why we take up serpents. It's better to always obey God."

"I don't think there should be any law against handling serpents in

... Surely the Lord's
anointed is before him.
1 Samuel, 16:6

Sister Langham lovingly cradles a fearsome serpent in her arms during church services in Micco, West Virginia. Bishop Kelly Williams stands by her side. "If West Virginia passed a law against serpent handling, I'd take them up anyhow," stresses Sister Langham. "It's better to obey God's law than man's. The laws of God are more important to follow in this kind of situation. I'd be willing to go to jail for doing God's Word, for following His law."
Photo by Brother Willie E. Sizemore.

church. I don't think there *really* is a law against it. The Tennessee law was passed to guard against endangering other people's lives," explains Brother Robert Grooms. "If you handle them yourself, you're not endangering anyone else's life. Now, if I throw the serpents at you, then I'm endangering your life. As far as me handling them, I've not broken any law. I believe in handling them right. I won't hand a serpent to anybody. And I don't want anybody in the church handing it to anybody else, unless they are anointed. They have to reach for the serpent and take it from whoever's got it. I say if it does get to the Supreme Court, they will rule that we have our rights."

"They try us for taking up serpents, yet they say, 'Well, you can bring your strychnine and set it up in church.' I don't think they should have the right to do this! What in the world gives them the right to

     . . . and they shall keep my laws
and my statutes in all mine
assemblies . . .

                  Ezekiel, 44:24

    Brother Gene Sherbert of the Holiness Church of God in Jesus Name, Kingston, Georgia, goes heavily under the anointing power. "The Bible says you need a school teacher 'til you get out of school, and you need a doctor 'till you can come to the Great Physician," explains Brother Gene. "You need a doctor to take care of you until you can get enough faith in the Great Physician, which is Jesus."
Photo by the authors.

decide that serpents are endangering lives, but strychnine isn't?" Brother Everett Fraley has pondered this question for years, and he feels frustrated at his inability to do anything about it, to get anyone of influence to listen to him. "They've just got it in for religious serpent handling. I think it's plain unfair. It's against a man's religious faith. I think a man should have the right to worship God the way he pleases. Let God anoint him for anything He wants to. They're playing a dangerous game with God when they fight against the anointing. After all, we never do anything that isn't in the Bible."

North Carolina simply considers serpent handling a public nuisance. Kentucky is the only Southeastern state which clearly and specifically outlaws the use of any reptiles (not just poisonous) in religious services. Their law doesn't say a person can't handle snakes during a picnic in his backyard or in a public park. Is it overlooked so long as a Bible isn't on the premises, a sermon being preached, or the name of Jesus being exhorted? Kentucky's law is, without comparison, the most unfair and prejudicial of them all.

Alabama, Tennessee, and Virginia say serpents can't be handled if it "endangers the life or health of *any* person." The interpretation of the law in these three states is the crux of the problem. The courts have blatantly fined and sentenced church people to jail for handling serpents when it is obvious to many that no one's life or health was being endangered. Even the court testimony of Tennessee's most recent star witness, Ed Ashburn, a Tennessee Bureau of Investigation (TBI) agent, proved as much. The law, worded as it is, can be and is misused at any given time to punish a small segment of the citizenry who have no political muscle, nor the monetary means to fight back.

The machinations of the judicial machinery in Cocke County, Tennessee, are a prime example of justice being miscarried to the extreme. Action was and is being taken to stop the serpent handlers in the tiny church just outside of Newport. Why? Because serpent handling is honestly believed to be a dangerous practice? Because outsiders (visitors) will be accidentally killed or hurt? Because the anointed put their snakes on others? Because they make unwilling members take up serpents to prove or test their faith? No! The reasoning and logic is ludicrous to say the least. The scholarly words of District Attorney General Henry F. Swann and Judge George R. Shepherd beautifully capsulize the motivation "What will it look like for Newport, if this isn't stopped?"

"We can't have Newport, called the snake handling capitol of the world!"

12

To Seek or Not To Seek
Medical Attention

... I say unto you, he that believeth on me hath everlasting life.
St. Joh,n 6:47

But I fear, lest by any means, as
the serpent beguiled Eve through his
subtility, so your minds should be
corrupted from the simplicity that is
in Christ.
2 Corinthians, 11:3

"No, I wouldn't go to a doctor if I were serpent bitten. I wouldn't
want to, really, I wouldn't want to. I'd just love to suffer it out. I'd
try," offers Sister Thelma Whittaker. "I'd try to be healed by God. I'd
love for all the saints (church members) to be with me and pray with
me. I'd love to suffer it out. I believe you're going to take it like God
wants you to anyhow. I believe He knows what you can endure, what
pain this body can stand. He knows, because He says He wouldn't put

any more upon you than you can bear. So, I think, if He would permit a serpent to bite you, He knows if you could suffer it out or not."

"I would pray that God gives me the faith that I wouldn't go to a doctor if I were serpent bitten, or sick from anything," reveals Sister Mary Bailey. She candidly goes on, "But really, I honestly don't know what I would do. But I have asked God, should I ever get bitten by a serpent, I have asked Him to give me the faith that I could rely on the prayers of the saints. I would just want them all to pray for me. I believe God would heal me."

"I had been in the hospital on three different occasions with an attack of kidney stones. They wanted to operate on me, but I never would let them," says Reverend Floyd McCall. "I knew the Lord had a time and a place where He would heal me. So, I really wasn't worried about it all. One night in church, I was healed. That was my last attack of kidney stones. I knew I was healed as soon as it happened. Others knew it too, because the Holy Ghost witnessed through them. God told them that I had just been healed. They came over and mentioned it to me. I said, 'Yes, I know I was just healed by the Lord.' I believe we should wait on the Lord to move. We should place our faith in Him rather than doctors."

"God give you the faith. He has to give you the faith when you are sick, or even if you take a serpent bite. If you didn't want to trust in God, you'd go to a doctor." Lida Davis is a woman who sincerely believes in faith healing and the power of God. She has good reason for her convictions, for this lady has been healed of a serious heart condition. "God will give you enough faith to trust in Him to take care of you, if you are serpent bit. I would love to, just like Brother Richard Williams, I'd love to 'lay on them old stones' and trust God like Brother Williams did."

"I have not gone to a doctor whenever I've been serpent bit, because the anointing was there and I knew it." Brother Willie Sizemore feels strongly about the choice of running to a doctor for help or simply putting his trust in God. He feels if his bite comes during the anointing, then God has permitted it to happen for a reason. "I believe God let it bite me. I didn't go to a doctor because I had faith in God's power. The faith I have is nothing more than a gift of God. Sometimes people have the faith, sometimes they don't. When I received a serpent bite from a copperhead, we had victory in the church. There was victory there in the church. I had strong enough faith to suffer the serpent bite. I knew I had it. By victory in the church, I mean everything was there. The Spirit was right. There was no fear. None whatsoever. The Spirit was there for everyone. We were all under a heavy anointing. Brother Richard Williams had already been bitten. God sent the faith right then that everyone would be all right. I started leading a song, and the Lord moved on us. There wasn't any fear of the bite or the serpents at all. So you see, that's what I mean about having the faith; we had the faith that it was okay."

The Lord recompense thy work,
and a full reward be given
thee . . .

Ruth, 2:12

Sister Lucille Dishner of Athens, West Virginia. Next to her is her daughter, wife of Brother John Holbrook. "If you get serpent bitten and don't have enough faith to stand up under the pain, then you had better go to a doctor right then, not later," warns Sister Lucille. "There's no sense of waiting until two or three days later and then making this decision. You're already in bad shape then. The doctor can't do much for you."

Photo by the authors.

"You've got to have faith in God and have faith in God's people's prayers to be healed. If you have this kind of faith, He'll heal you," states Brother Robert Fraley. He would like to say he'd have enough faith to be healed through God's power. Brother Bob would ask the people to pray for him and hope that he'd be healed. But this man feels nobody really knows what they'd do until a specific situation arises. People say what they'd *like* to do, or *think* they'd do, but one never really knows until he actually gets sick or hurt and needs help. "I have sought medical attention before. It depends on the time you'd be sick. Maybe you just feel like your faith is weak. Maybe you've been down in the valley, and maybe you just don't feel you're worthy of God's healing. Or maybe you don't feel you could pray through to God to get the help you need. Then, you should seek medical help. But if you've been living close to God, praying to Him daily, and fasting, then if you had an accident or got sick in some way, you'd feel maybe close enough to God that you'd feel certain He'd heal. It's really the state of mind you happen to be in when something like this happens to you."

"If I was snake bitten under an anointment of God, I would try not to go to a doctor. The first thing I'd do is fall on my face and ask God to let me live and to heal me," suggests Brother Ralph Eslinger. "It depends on faith. If I could keep my faith up, I sure wouldn't go. But if my faith began to come down, I would go to a doctor. I'd try to first have faith. I'd call the elders of the church to lay hands on me and pray for me. If God didn't move on me, I'd go to the doctor."

"I didn't go to any doctor when I was bitten by a rattlesnake. I wanted to put my faith in the Lord for healing and protection." Billy Jay Forrester suffered horribly for many days after his serpent bite. He says the devil tried to plant fear and doubt in his mind by suggesting death was imminent. But this young man kept his mind "on the Lord," and the fear was removed. "I was afraid I'd lose my arm or hand, maybe, if I went to the doctor. I'd rather have kept my faith in the Lord than lose my arm. The doctor might have wanted to cut if off. I do feel the Lord moved and took care of me. He healed me. I have no doubt about it."

"If I was anointed when I took up the serpent and it bit me, I don't believe I would go to a doctor. I believe the Lord would take care of me. If I just took one up on faith and got bit, I don't know what I'd do then. I might just go to one. I probably wouldn't ever take one up on faith. I know it takes the anointing." Brother Everett Fraley has had quite a long association with serpent handling churches. He uses the example of Roscoe Mullins to show what can happen when medical attention is preferred over God's ability to heal. "Mullins has one hand missing. He's got just a part of his arm. He lost it by a rattlesnake bite. Mullins was taken to a doctor after be passed out. His family took him. He didn't go of his own free will. Roscoe knew nothing about it until he woke up in the hospital. They ended up taking his hand off. To the

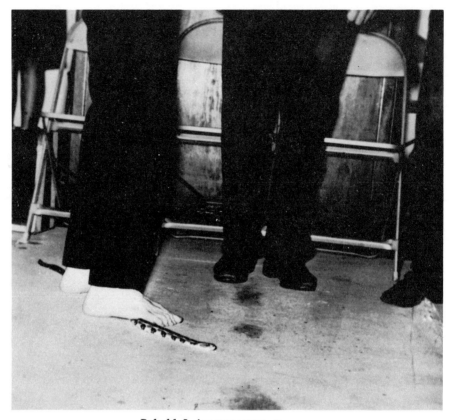

Behold, I give you power to
tread on serpents . . .
                    St. Luke, 10:19

Reverend Alfred Ball. Brother Al took off his shoes and daringly walked barefoot on this live poisonous snake. That same night, Brother Clyde was bitten on the heel and passed out. After hands were laid upon him and a special healing prayer was offered, he regained consciousness and quickly recovered.
Courtesy of the Newport Plain Talk.

best of my knowledge, he didn't wait on the Lord to move — he went right on to the doctor."

"I would trust in the Lord to be healed of cancer. I would pray and seek. But now, I don't really find fault with doctors. Sometimes I'll go to doctors myself. But if I get sick, I seek God first for deliverance. If He won't heal me, then I do something else. If I do not get healed, I would go to a doctor." Brother Robert Grooms believes he should give the Lord a chance to move on him. He sincerely feels a doctor and God don't mix. Robert feels God will not work along with a doctor. "If

Be ye therefore followers of God as
dear children. And walk in love . . .
Ephesians, 5:1-2

Reverend Carl Porter, the dynamic pastor of the Holiness Church of God in Jesus Name, Kingston, Georgia. "When a serpent bites you, don't go picking around on it," warns Brother Porter. "Don't mess with it. You can set up gangrene, you can set up poisoning. Just leave it alone. If it takes one day or twenty days to heal, just leave it be, and God'll heal it. He'll heal it in His own time."
Photo by the authors.

you're going to use one of them, you've got to lay the other one down. I simply go by my own feelings, and everybody I've talked to feels the same way. It's all what you put your faith and trust in. If I put my trust in the Lord, then the Lord's going to heal me. If I put my trust in a doctor, that doctor's what cures you. I have trusted the Lord and He's delivered me many times. What I do is I say 'God, if it's Your will, now You heal me.' I wait on the Lord, and if God don't heal me, – then I seek help from a doctor. God might not want to heal me because of something I've done. He's chastising me. If I'm going to get any ease, I'm going to have to step out and do it myself. Most of the time, sickness is on people because they don't obey the Lord. I used to suffer a lot more than I do now. It was only because I was disobedient unto God. I wouldn't get out and do His work. When I got willing to step out and do His bidding, I was all right."

At times, these practitioners will resort to medicines and doctors for some health problems while fully intending to rely on God for others. For instance, "A lot of people ask why we would take aspirin or cough syrup for a bad cold, but wouldn't take aspirin to relieve the pain of a serpent bite," said smiling Richard Williams. "But, when I'm handling a serpent, I'm doing that strictly in obedience to the Word of God. I feel God will give me strength to endure, and a serpent bite is a lot worse than a bad cold! It seems during the other illnesses, not being exactly in obedience to the Word, the faith isn't there."

Richard went on to voice the prevailing fear of snake bite victims. "When a person gets serpent bitten and suffers it out, there are no marks, no scars, and they can use their limbs. But if they go to a doctor, he'll cut that arm from one end to the other, or cut it all the way off."

Brother Richard's conviction that God is Creator of all things led him to ask, "Why should a person go to a secondhanded element for their healing, when they can have the firsthanded element which is God? I try to pray for God's will to be done – not what *I* want done, but what the *Lord* wants done. I pray, 'If you want him to live, spare him. If it's Your will for him to go on out, give him grace and strength to go on out in the Lord.' If you don't have the faith to suffer out a sickness, then you have to do the next best thing, and that's go to a doctor. As your faith is, so be it."

The ideal healer would use the natural herbs of the fields for his medicinal compounds. He would employ nature's own existing secrets of recovery. This approach to giving aid and relief would be more easily accepted by the faithful, for such a man was Luke, the physician friend of Jesus.

Relief, however, is not usually sought, particularly by snake bite victims. Suffering is a purification process through which ties to God are strengthened. Bishop Kelly Williams hopes he can suffer through any affliction. "I've never taken a pill or rubbed anything on a serpent bite. God has taken care of me." The West Virginia Bishop will not say for sure, though, what he will do when the next one bites him. "It takes faith, and I don't want to boast ahead of time." He goes on to explain the importance of suffering. "We are in the learning stages of suffering. In the end, the real church is really going to suffer. We are being trained to suffer, so when it does come, we'll be in shape to cope with it. God gets His glory out of the suffering we do for Him."

Everyone "hopes to endure." They are comforted by the fact that their brothers and sisters in the faith are willing to pray and lay hands in the hour of need. These prayers are often reported to bring temporary relief as a crisis runs its course, as well as subsequent healing. "I know that if somebody gets bitten up here (Ohio or West Virginia)," "Brother Richard Williams says, "the saints will stay with him. I've stayed and prayed with people for three days."

The Spirit of the Lord is
upon me, because he hath
anointed me . . .
                    St. Luke, 4:18

Sister Eunice Ball of Newport, Tennessee. "The most wonderful doctor of all is
Jesus," believes Sister Eunice. "If I have strong enough faith, I don't ever have to go
to a doctor. God won't ever let me suffer more than I can stand to suffer. He will
always take care of me. It's in the Word. I have faith in God's power to heal. Any
suffering I do will bring me down closer to Jesus."
Photo by the authors.

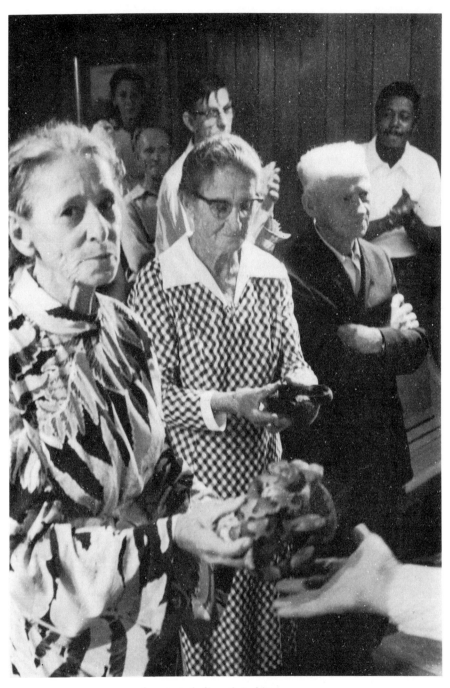

... whosoever believeth in him
should not perish ...
John, 3:16

Sister Edna Clanton and Sister Belle Whitworth of Greenville, South Carolina. "We believe God is able to do anything," declares Sister Whitworth. "That's what it all really boils down to. When God moves, there's no such thing as a fiery serpent." *Photo by the authors.*

This world contains many more unbelievers and weak believers than those of the deeper faith. The doctors are here for them. The very presence of doctors is a manifestation of God's grace Brother Ralph Spence suggests, "God, which is love and nothing but love, shows His mercy by giving those without that faith relief from their afflictions through the knowledge He has given to the doctors."

By faith the serpents are handled, and by faith their crippling bites are healed. By faith the strychnine is swallowed, and by faith the poison is washed away. But faith is not of man and cannot be called up at a moment's notice. Richard Williams revealed, "Faith is a gift of God. He gives it to you when you need it most."

13

The Miracle of Healing—

Laying On of Hands

Wherefore I put thee in remembrance
that thou stir up the gift of God,
which is in thee by the putting on
of my hands.

> 2 Timothy, 1:6

And we are his witnesses of these
things; and so is also the Holy Ghost,
who God hath given to them that obey
him.

> The Acts, 5:32

Is any sick among you? let him call for the elders of the church; and let
them pray over him, anointing him with oil in the name of the Lord: And the
prayer of faith shall save the sick, and the Lord shall raise him up; . . .

> James, 5:14-15

This Biblical passage suggests that there are on earth today apostles
and prophets who possess the same power and authority which were
available in the days of Christ. The Holiness serpent handlers, along

with all other fundamentalists, are convinced the Bible is the living Word. To them, it is every bit as appropriate for the believers of the space age as it was for the followers of yesterday.

The very emblem of the healing arts was developed from the Old Testament (Numbers, 21:8). The Caduceus, serpents intertwined on a pole or staff, immediately suggests scientific medical aid. Its spiritual origin and meaning have almost been forgotten.

However, to Reverend Floyd McCall, the serpent's role in healing will long be remembered. This soft-spoken preacher was attending services one night at a sister church in Carson Springs, Tennessee. He was suffering a great deal with kidney stones at the time, and was experiencing severe pain that evening.

"God told me if I would obey Him, He'd heal me" recalled Brother Floyd. "I didn't know what He meant. That's all the Lord spoke, 'If you'll obey me, I'll heal you.' "

Presently, another brother announced there was a new copperhead in the church. He suggested that if anyone felt the anointing of God and would obey Him, they could handle it.

"It hit me right then and there what God meant when He spoke to me. So I took up the new copperhead. The serpent *did* bite me. Then I began to wonder in my mind, 'Lord, is this what you meant? You told me to obey You, and now, I've done got bit because of it.' The Lord then spoke to me clearly and said, 'You're healed.' And I knew it — the Lord moved on me."

Robert Fraley tells of a miracle wrought through a child's simple faith. When he was a youngster in Big Stone Gap, Virginia, he picked up an unexploded firecracker, which promptly went off in his hand. Brother Bob vividly remembers the unbearable pain. "I fell on my knees and said, 'Lord, heal me.' I was a small child and didn't really know how to pray. I just said, 'Lord, Heal me.' I felt that burn and hurt go out the end of my fingers. It left instantly. I went in the house and washed the powder off my hands."

On the day after Christmas in 1967, a doctor told Lida Davis of Williamson, West Virginia, she had two years to live. "He told me only one side of my heart was working properly. I don't know if I'd had a heart attack or what, but I know something serious had happened to me. I couldn't drive my car, and I couldn't walk — I could only slide my feet. He made an appointment to send me to a good heart specialist in Huntington. But I just told him, if I was going to die, I was going to die! I didn't want to be a guinea pig.

"I went to church one night, and the Word was being preached. God came right down on me. It was just like lightning flashing in the sky. It hit me in the top of my head and went down. When it got to my heart, it seemed like my heart went out. When it came back, it came back in place, and the 'lightning' went out my feet.

"I went back to the doctor. He X-rayed me, and checked me

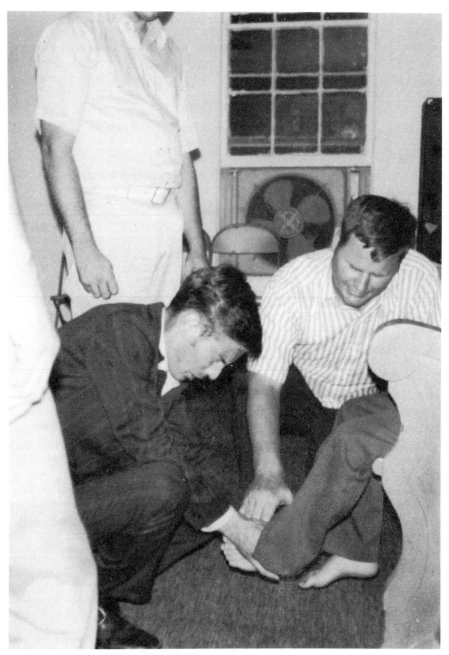

*Every good gift and every perfect
gift is from above . . .*
James, 1:17

Brother Alfred Ball calling on the Lord to heal a child's injured foot during services at the Holiness Church of God in Jesus Name, Carson Springs, Tennessee. Brother Al went to jail that night after the service was over. "Blood poisoning had set in and the boy was crying with the pain from it. He was limping and couldn't put any weight on his foot. The next day, Robbie hollared up from the walk in front of my cell and said his foot was better. He seemed to be feeling better after the prayer. God must have healed him."
Photo by Jackie Eslinger.

thoroughly. I had an electrocardiogram done. He told me he couldn't find anything wrong with my heart. So, I know God moved. God has healed me. There's no doubt about it in my mind. God gave me the faith to trust Him."

These Jesus people give the credit where credit is due — to God. All are aware it is not the preacher or the others praying and laying on hands who achieve the positive results. Some of the ministers do feel they have a God-given gift for healing the sick. Their repeated successes convince them of their special calling. But Richard Williams, an amazingly productive emissary of God, did not claim the gift of healing.

"To have the gift of healing, you'd have to be qualified. It's a gift that God has to give you. I believe when God gives the gift of healing, you can heal anybody you want to. If you have the gift of healing, there can be no failure to that. And, to get the gift, you'd have to be close enough to God to heal only those *He told* you to heal.

"Now, the Holy Ghost will move and do that work without you having the gift. The Holy Ghost we have in us will heal at various times. When God wants a person healed, He'll give us the Holy Ghost and the power."

Are preachers or proven healers the only ones who need to pray for the sick? "No," emphasized Brother Richard, "any believer of the Gospel can lay hands on the sick. The people are merely the contacts with God. If I want something from God, I can get down and talk with God. But then again, a still greater contact is the prayers of an entire church membership."

Bishop Kelly Williams, pastor of the Full Gospel Jesus Church, Micco, West Virginia, has had a glorious healing career in over twenty years of preaching. One incident involved the use of a prayer cloth.

Prayer cloths are an ancient healing implement, dating back to the time of the apostle Paul. He prayed over aprons and cloths and sent them to people in need. He would pray that the spiritual power would accompany the cloths.

"We don't feel that a cloth can do anything for anybody," assures Bishop Kelly. "It's the Spirit that accompanies it."

There was a married woman in California who was unhappy over her inability to have children. The doctor had told her she would never be able to conceive. Grasping every thread of hope, she wrote her sister who was a member of the Micco church. This woman requested that they anoint a prayer cloth and send it to her in California. She wanted the church to ask the Lord to let her bear a child.

"We waited for the right anointing, a good moving of the Spirit, and then we prayed over a cloth," related Richard Williams. "We sent that prayer cloth to the woman in California. Ten months later, she wrote back that she had given birth to a big, healthy boy, and they were both fine. She gave God all the praise. She gave our saints praise, because she had confidence that their prayers and the Spirit and the name Jesus

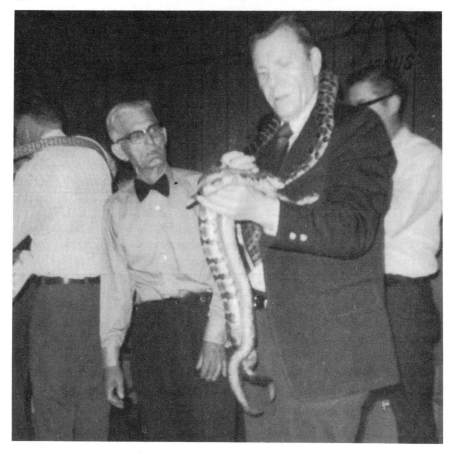

God is a spirit and they that
worship him, must worship him
in spirit and in truth.

St. John, 4:24

Bishop Kelly Williams during services at the Full Gospel Jesus Church in Micco, West Virginia. Intently looking on is Brother Enos Sizemore. "Amen, praise the Lord. God will touch that sister's body, even though she's in bad condition," says Kelly, in reference to a hospitalized church member. "I told her to hold her faith, hold on to the Word of God, amen, praise the Lord. 'They shall lay hands on the sick and they shall recover.' That don't mean that you will jump up right now — but you will recover."
Photo by Sister Candis Blondine Williams.

that came with the cloth enabled her to become in the family way."

Some overt act as an example of the seeker's faith was required throughout the scriptures. One excellent illustration of this can be found in II Kings, 5:14-19, when the leper was asked to show his belief by dipping himself seven times in the Jordan river. Often today, the expression of faith is the simple act of going forward in the church. Or the afflicted person may approach a pastor privately and offer one's self for the healing. Likewise, the one who intends to perform the blessing prepares himself, usually by prayer and fasting.

"I fast for other people and for the church. I expect greater benefits and more spiritual power from it," states Willie Sizemore, "I believe fasting takes you a whole lot closer to God. It makes you more spiritual."

"We teach that if people would fast for one meal a day — a meal they would ordinarily eat — God will bless them that much more." Richard Williams fasted regularly. The longest time this 200 pound evangelist fasted was six days. "We like to emphasize a three day fast, because in the Bible they would call a three day fast for the church. This means eat nothing for three days. It's hard for people who work, but we do it."

The faithful believe God rewards prayer and fasting with a commensorate amount of grace, honor, and spiritual power. For the humility of prayer, God bestows His blessings. For the sacrifice of fasting, God sends the power, the anointing to heal.

In Alfred Ball's case, the anointing to pray for the sick, to lay on hands, to heal is very close to the strength of that for casting out devils.[1] His hands become extremely numb, they tingle, and they draw somewhat. "It goes all the way up into my arms," explains Al. "I can feel it in my face. My tongue is numb. And my mouth feels numb and dry inside. It's a very strong anointing."

Reverend Ball is considered a successful conduit for God's healing power. There are innumerable willing witnesses to the positive results of this man's healing prayers. In 1966, a woman came to the Community House of Prayer where Brother Alfred was leading a revival. She had been troubled with kidney problems and chest pains. Some time later, Mrs. Tammie Dunbar wrote, "Brother Ball prayed for me, and the Lord touched my body and healed me completely. The swelling left my feet, and the pains left my chest and stomach. I can't thank God enough for what He has done for me. Praise the Lord. Thank you, Jesus."

That same year, a lady took her granddaughter Janet to Alfred for prayer. He was holding a service at the Little Mission in Hot Springs, North Carolina. The child was a victim of rheumatic fever when only three years old. She was left with a serious heart murmur and couldn't run and play with other kids. Little Janet had been under a doctor's care for the past few years. She had been going to the Rheumatic Fever Clinic in Ashville. The fervent supplications of this sincere young preacher were not in vain. The grandmother, Mrs. Ernest Holt, reported,

---

[1]The term demons is never used in Appalachian Holiness churches.

"When I took her back to the clinic for a check-up, the doctor couldn't find anything wrong with her. He said she could play or do anything she wanted to do. I thank God for this, because I know that He can heal, if we have enough faith in Him."

Brother Al's prayers are loud and commanding. "Lord, I will not accept anything but healing!" Or, they are silently intense as he closes his eyes tightly and lays his hands on the head of the sufferer.

"When you feel like there's any certain time for you to come for prayer," Brother Al invites his congregation, "you get up and come right then. Don't wait. Come right then."

Endless stories of miraculous healing can be told by Christians in all faiths. There are many medical professionals who are willing to acknowledge some recovery incidents as being beyond logical scientific explantion. They easily profess the intervention of a powerful and healing God. Still, some staunch scientists refuse to view miracles as anything but happy coincidences. That divine intervention would accomplish something medical research could not is incomprehensible to them. The question remains: Is not the coincidence often as miraculous as the healing?

Bishop Kelly Williams doesn't wonder. He believes. "It's what I *know* God can do."

14

Casting Out the Spirits of Satan

... they brought unto him many that
were possessed with devils: and he
cast out the spirits with his word,
and healed all that was sick.
St. Matthew, 8:16

And these signs shall follow them
that believe: In my name shall they
cast out devils . . .
St. Mark, 16:17

Reverend Alfred Ball is a tall, slender mountain preacher who believes his main calling in the ministry is for casting out devil spirits. He is a true exorcist in every sense of the word. And he is a sincere and devout Christian who practices what he preaches. Brother Al, as he is fondly referred to by friends, helps pastor the rather isolated little church buried in a heavily wooded hollow on English Mountain in East Tennessee. Exorcisms are frequently carried out successfully at this house of the Lord.

"The anointing power comes from the Holy Ghost, from God, to cast out an evil spirit from somebody who is possessed. There are many different types of evil spirits," says Brother Alfred. "One kind is epilepsy. This *is* an evil spirit force, a devil in disguise. I have cast them out of many people, and they have never again had a seizure that I personally knew anything about.

"One lady I know had epilipsy for seventeen years and was on the strongest medication they give people for this. She was still having at least one seizure a day," explains Reverend Ball. "One night in a service, God anointed me to cast out devils, and she came up for prayer. She didn't tell me what was wrong with her. I immediately discerned by the Spirit of God and by the anointing that this was a spirit of the devil in her. An unclean spirit. I didn't know exactly what kind it was, and I didn't ask. I just began to rebuke this evil spirit and commanded it to come out of her. After a period of time, it did. I kept praying with her until the evil force left her body.

"Then there are religious types of evil spirits. They'll come to church and sing with everybody else. They'll shout. They'll get on the floor and dance or jump 'in the Spirit,' supposedly," states Al. "Yet, if you walk outside the church, you might hear them cussin'. They'll do anything that any sinner-person would do. And yet, they'll come to church and claim to live right. This is a *religious* type devil. It deceives somebody into thinking they're really a Christian, and they'll die and be lost. That's just one of Satan's many tricks."

Robert Fraley is a regular member of the Holiness Church of God in Jesus Name. His father is the pastor of such a church in Big Stone Gap, Virginia. Brother Bob has witnessed many authentic exorcism rituals. He reveals: "I've seen people prayed for, and they would later say the devil was cast out of them. There's a young girl in Big Stone Gap, who rushed up to the altar while praying for the Holy Ghost. Two or three of God's people already filled with the Holy Ghost laid their hands on her. She finally let out a horrible, loud scream. When the scream left, she started speaking in other tongues. This girl later testified that is *was* a devil cast out of her. And when the devil went out, the Holy Ghost came in. She said the devil scratched her throat badly when it came up and out of her."

"I've seen many people come up front in church. They want prayer for healing a specific thing. The Lord tells me when any of these people have a devil in them. Casting out devils is a strange thing." Reverend Floyd McCall has had lots of experience in casting devils out of people. He feels the devil has the person bound, and is really the cause of their problems. "The devil is over their life, in control of it. I do know, just about every time, what specific devil has got the person bound. Either it's a sexual devil, or it's a suicide devil. There are a lot of ways a devil can bind people. The Lord always lets me know exactly how to pray for them. He tells me what direction to go in. He leads me to the correct way of beating the devil spirit in the person."

How does a preacher know when someone is possessed of a devil or unclean spirit? According to Reverend Robert Grooms, it's the way the person acts and reacts. "When you start to pray for them, you can actually feel the evil force coming against you. It's just like praying against something, and you have trouble getting through. It's like pushing up against a brick wall. You are simply stuck there! If you ask God for more of His power — if you get power enough to cast it out — the devil *has* to come forth. It *absolutely must* come out of the possessed person. Sometimes they come out screaming, sometimes crying. Sometimes they make the person bite and claw you. Sometimes they try to kill you. God has often used me to cast devils out of people in my church."

"I have a cold, chilly, harsh feeling come over my body when I come up against someone who has the devil spirits in them," reveals Brother Ralph Eslinger. "They've not got a child of God deceived. They may have somebody that don't know the real Spirit of God deceived. But they can't fool a true child of God. I can discern the devil's spirit that's working in people. When I feel it, I commence praying for them."

"You are commanded in the name of Jesus to leave!"

"I rebuke you in the Spirit of God!"

"Devil — come out! In Jesus name!"

"You must come out! By the blood of Jesus — out!"

"By the power of God — you *will* come out!"

These are typical phrases used in various exorcism rites. All agree that the deliverer has to sternly command the devil to come out of the possessed person. He can't command God to do anything. But, as for the devil, God gives the faithful the power and the authority to command him to come forth.

Sometimes, entire congregations will hurriedly leave the church when an exorcism is going to be undertaken. They patiently, sometimes fearfully, wait outside until it's all over. When the devil finally leaves the possessed person, he or she must continually "pray and seek the Lord." This is done as a protective measure designed to stop Satan from regaining control of the mind and body. Most of the faithful are afraid the devil will try to enter and possess them. All church members believe that the evil spirit promptly seeks out someone else to take control of. It's supposed to be impossible for the spirit of the devil to be in possession of a baptized person who also has the Holy Ghost.

"Sometimes I have prayed for people and scared everybody to death. They all got up and left. They ran outside and peeked in through the windows. I stayed right there and prayed on and on. I just kept commanding the devil to come out in Jesus name. When he did finally come out, the person just passed out on the floor." Brother Grooms is always determined to win out over the forces of evil. He refuses to give up, no matter how long it takes, until he feels deliverance come to the possessed person. "Most people come up saying they're sick. But they're actually possessed of an evil spirit that's got them in a shape that makes them think they're sick. And really, after a while of thinking you're sick, you will be sick. When they come forward to be prayed for, I know the minute I touch them whether they're sick or possessed of an evil spirit."

In order to be delivered, a person would usually have to acknowledge that they were possessed by an evil spirit. They must actively seek deliverence. But there are exceptions to this. A minister may discern the evil spirit in them and call the individual to come up to the altar for prayer. They must be willing to admit they are in fact possessed, or at least, they must realize it is something they have no control over. Then the person can usually be set free through the exhausting exorcism ritual.

"I have seen many people obsessed by a devil. Obsessed simply means that the devil spirit is around them just waiting to come inside and take possession," explains Brother Ralph Eslinger. "Possessed means that the devil's already on the inside and in control of the person. A legion of devils looks like a flock of blackbirds, or maybe sometimes a ball of fire. Sometimes they even look like a serpent crawling across the floor of the church. You *can* see these spirits with your spiritual eyes, when they actually leave a possessed person. But you must be in the anointed state in order to experience this phenomenon."

Exorcism is by no means new to many of the more fundamentalist churches throughout the United States. It has always been an important part of their worship, and it has been openly practiced, but widely ignored by others. It comes as no surprise to people such as Ball, Fraley, McCall, Grooms, and Eslinger, when they hear tales of devil casting now taking place in some of the more liberally oriented churches. Even the best-selling *Exorcist* wasn't a shocker to any of these Christians. They have experienced, many times over, the power of Satan in combat against the power of their living God. To them and their fathers before them, devil possession has always been a reality. It is taught in the Bible, and it must be believed. For the Bible, in their own words, "is the inspired Word of God." And this is never doubted.

15

Speaking in Tongues—Glossolalia

> For he that speaketh in an unknown
> tongue, speaketh not unto men, but
> unto God: for no man understandeth
> him . . . he speaketh mysteries.
> 1 Corinthians, 14:2

> . . . the Holy Ghost came on them;
> and they spake with tongues, and
> prophesied.
> The Acts, 19:6

"I speak in tongues, I believe, direct to God. A lot of people get the tongues mixed up. The *gift* of tongues comes *from* the Holy Ghost. There's only one Spirit, but there are different manifestations of that one Spirit. All the gifts come from the same Spirit which is the Holy Ghost." Brother Robert Fraley feels no confusion in his way of understanding tongues. "My speaking in tongues *is not* the 'gift' of tongues. It is the Holy Ghost — direct to God. The 'gift' of tongues *can* be interpreted. The 'gift' is either interpreted by someone else or by the speaker, himself. This is for the edification of the church. It's when God wants to tell the church something or give the church instruction.

Maybe it's to help the church in some way."

"There are a lot of people in my church who speak in tongues. I can interpret what they are saying. When I interpret, I tell the congregation word for word what they are saying," says Reverend Robert Grooms. "I feel tongues are a special message given by God to a member of the church. God told a man in the congregation one time, He said, 'I've strived and I've strived with you.' God will get tired of striving. I feel I have the gift of interpreting tongues, but not the gift of speaking in tongues. I never did *desire* the gift of speaking in tongues. But I could get it by praying for it."

"If you have the Holy Ghost, you *have* to speak in tongues. Everyone who has the Holy Ghost speakes in tongues, but everyone who speaks in tongues doesn't necessarily have the Holy Ghost. If it's the *real* tongues, then the person does have the Holy Ghost. You would have to have the genuine Holy Ghost yourself to be able to know the difference. You then *can* tell the difference between those who really have the Holy Ghost and are speaking in real tongues and those who are faking it." Reverend Willie E. Sizemore often speaks in tongues. He is quick to acknowledge that some people put on an act and are not really inspired by the Holy Ghost.

Why does this devout man speak in tongues? "The Holy Ghost controls my tongue. The Spirit of God speaks through me. I speak in tongues for the same reason I handle serpents. It's really quite simple to understand. I do it because it's one of the five signs, that's all. That's the only reason I do it. He said, 'They shall speak with new tongues,' in Mark, 16:17. It's not *our* purpose. Speaking in tongues is not our purpose at all. The Word of God just says that we would do it. I never asked the Lord about it, I never asked Him why, because I don't have to. It's simply the Word of God — it's one of the five signs. Speaking in tongues and the interpretation of tongues are also given us as spiritual gifts. You can find this clearly mentioned in I Corinthians, 12:10."

"I have to get a special anointing in my mouth to speak in tongues. It's a real good feeling when the Holy Ghost moves on me and takes control of my tongue," reveals Brother Everett Fraley. "I don't get any special feeling in my arms when I speak in tongues, like I do for laying on hands to heal. The gift of tongues should always be interpreted. If somebody stands up in church and speaks in an unknown tongue and it is not interpreted, someone in the congregation has disobeyed God. The person who was speaking should pray for an interpretation. If it's not interpreted, then I would assume it wasn't really the gift of tongues. The gift of tongues is to edify the church, to be spoken for the good of the church, or someone in the congreagation."

"Some of the sisters and brothers in this faith speak in tongues," says Sister Bea Eslinger. "Sometimes they speak in tongues directly to God. This is not to be interpreted in church."

"Speaking in tongues should always be interpreted according to the

Take heed unto thyself, and unto the doctrine;
continue in them: for in doing this thou shalt
both save thyself, and them that hear thee.
I Timothy, 4:16

Sister Gladys Kilgore, pastor Carl Porter's aunt, at church in Kingston, Georgia. "The anointing of God, it comes through love. There is no fear," explains Sister Gladys. "There's no fear at all when I do this. You just don't even think the serpents can harm you in any way. Normally, I'm afraid of snakes. I stay away from them unless the anointing of God is on me."
Photo by the authors.

scriptures," states Reverend Al Ball. "However, there is a lot that is never interpreted. It should be interpreted by the person speaking or by someone else in the church. There is a gift of tongues and a gift of interpretation of tongues."

Floyd McCall says, "The Lord works through you to do it. You know when you're doing it, because God wouldn't let you do something without realizing you're doing it. Tongues is a sign to the unbelievers. They don't understand it. It takes a person with the Holy Ghost and the knowledge of God to understand the mystery of tongues. It is to let people know what the Spirit is speaking about. If you speak in tongues, Paul says to pray that you can interpret it."

"There are different tongues," suggests Reverend Floyd McCall. 'New tongues' means you don't speak like you did when you were out in sin. You've got a new tongue, now. You don't say the things you used to say. 'Other tongues' are spoken direct to God. The Bible says no man can understand it."

For many decades, glossolalia has been an integral part of fundamental religions. The "mystery of tongues" as Reverend McCall said remains just that — a mystery. Reverend Richard Williams had an interesting approach to the subject of tongues. "I believe that with the gift of tongues, God will let you speak other languages. With the gift of interpretation, I would be able to interpret the various languages of the world. If the gifts would come, I believe I could speak and understand Spanish, French, German — all of them."

Amid varying ideas on the gifts of tongues and interpretation of tongues, there is one fact agreed upon by all Holiness believers. John Brown of Detroit, states it. "You speak in tongues as the Spirit gives utterance. It takes the Spirit of God to speak in tongues."

16

Not a Hair Was Singed

—Taking Up Fire

... the trial of your faith, being
much more precious than of gold ...
may be tried with fire ...
1 Peter, 1:7

... the fire had no power, nor was
an hair of their head singed, neither
were their coats changed, nor the
smell of the fire had passed on
them.
Daniel, 3:27

The Full Gospel Jesus Church of Columbus, Ohio, leaped to life with
the toe-tapping upbeat of "Gimme that old time religion ..." The
music drew enthusiastic singers like a magnet to the front of the bright
and spotless little sanctuary. One by one the "saints" (a term referring
to brothers and sisters of the faith) gathered in a semi-circle around the
pulpit. The clapping, jiving crescent of worshipers pressed closer

149

together and closer to God. The Spirit they were seeking began descending heavily. It was Fall and there were no serpents — it would be a good night to handle fire.

Pastor Willie Sizemore and his assistant pastor, Richard Williams, took turns preaching. The low-key, highly emotional, almost pleading style of Brother Sizemore was dramatically impressive. It was complimented by the whispery, floating melody from Brother Ralph Spence, who strummed his magic electric guitar softly, sweetly in the background. Willie ended this speaking session with a moving, heart-felt song, sung more to his Jesus than to his congregation.

Brother Richard now stepped forward. His sermon was begun in a normal tone of voice, but it rapidly worked up to a fevered pitch. He trotted around the front of the church and dashed up and down the aisle. Brother Richard was a most dynamic man of the cloth. He quickly worked up a sweat, and the rivulets of perspiration ran down his face. Throughout his spirited message, Richard frequently locked gazes with a saint who would nod in agreement or bounce out of his seat and cry, "Yeah! Yeah!" Hallelujahs and amens rang from the rafters.

Young Williams was a crowd pleaser, a showman whom everyone loved to hear. He always followed scripture closely but delighted in interpreting it understandably. He preached often in the vernacular. This night he described how John the Baptist would recognize Jesus when he approached for baptism: "God told John, He said, 'John, when the dove lights on his shoulder, that's my boy!' "

The church was singing again, a lively, jazzy song of love and adoration. Pastor Sizemore became anointed. He reached into the lectern and brought out the torch — a Pepsi bottle full of kerosene. There was a wad of cotton stuffed in its neck. He struck a match and touched it to the makeshift wick. The flame shot up, settled to about a foot in length, and burned steadily. The music drifted to a sing-song chant of "Have your way, Lord; have your way, God." Brother Willie cradled the torch under his arm like a football and cupped the flame in his hands.

The pastor continued this for about a minute, then shifted the torch to both hands, and held it under his chin. The six inch wide wall of fire licked at his shirt collar and earlobes. Slowly, tantalizingly, he moved it back and forth under his serenely smiling face for a full five minutes. He set the bottle on the pulpit, held his hands over the flame, and actively praised God.

With a quick squeeze of the wick, Brother Sizemore put out the fire with his fingers. The tempo stepped up immediately to praising, preaching, singing, and dancing. The jingle-jangle tambourines, the compelling guitars, the insistent drum beat maintained the spirit in exhilirating style.

Soon, Brother Williams became anointed and re-ignited the torch. He

... ye have purified your souls
in obeying the truth through
the Spirit ...

1 Peter, 1:22

Brother Billy Lemming, devout Christian serpent handler from Kingston, Georgia, holds a torch to his hand. "We go by the eleventh chapter of Hebrews where it says by faith the violence of fire is quenched," reveals Billy. "The violence of fire is the burning portion, the heat, the suffering. I hold back until God gives me a real good anointing."
Photo by the authors.

deliberately bathed both hands, finger by finger, in a seven inch spire of flame as he slowly paced the altar area. He then returned to behind the pulpit and grasped the sizzling hot bottle neck with one hand. He casually reached his other hand through the fire and lifted the wick farther out of the torch. The flame now blazed higher and wider as Richard seemed oblivious to the burning cotton particles clinging to his hand and fingers. With no apparent urgency, he flicked off the glowing bits. Brother Williams held the bottle in his right hand up close to his chest. While Richard stood there testifying, he gestured to the spellbound congregation with a blackened left forefinger. His face was completely framed in smoke and fire.

Brother Sizemore took the bottle from Richard and again calmly passed his hands through the twelve inch blaze. He then extended his arm and held the torch under his sleeve. "This fire *will* burn," he exclaimed. Instantly, the smell of burning fabric permeated the room. There was a hole the size of a quarter in the pastor's new shirt.

"Yes, Lord, yes, Jesus. This fire will burn."

Once more, Brother Richard took the torch. He clutched the flame to his breast and closed a streaked, sooty right hand around a pint jar of strychnine. With flames lapping at his throat, he gulped down about half of the deadly liquid. Richard stood the bottle on the pulpit. As if to attest to the divinity of the ritual, the torch sat like a fiery challenge and flickered for a moment in the perfect shape of a cross.

The flame was extinguished. The two preachers and Ralph Spence joked good-naturedly about Willie's shirt. Richard laughed, "Brother Willie, you wife's going to *kill* you."

The pastor grinned and said, "Yes, I ruin more shirts this way. She wonders sometimes why I always have to handle fire when I'm wearing a new one."

Sister Jacqueline, sincerely devout but a recent newcomer to the faith, smiled with obvious warmth and slight resignation.

More singing. More shouting. More fire.

A sister tried to light the torch. She broke one match, so Pastor Sizemore lit it for her. Again, the Pepsi bottle, now cloudy with smoke, made the rounds. This time, the women of the church who felt led to, came forward. They passed it among them, fanning their hands and arms through the blaze. Some were speaking in tongues. Others were murmuring prayers.

The sister who lit the torch handed it to one of the women who had joined the fervent cluster. She held the bottle at its base, her eyes closed tightly. Two other sisters thrust their fingers in and out of the fire, but the possessor remained motionless, whispering, praying. The seconds ticked away. The music faded. The flame danced in the sister's still hands and made ghostly shadows on her face.

In the twinkling of an eye, Brother Spence stepped from behind the pulpit. He quickly took the bottle from the sister, smothered the fire with his bare hands, and put the torch back inside the pulpit. Ralph slipped under the shoulder strap of his electric guitar and played the congregation back to reality.

The fire handlers pulled clean, white rags from the same area that housed the torch. They all wiped the smudges from their unseered hands, arms, and faces. There were no burns — no blisters. The service ended shortly thereafter. The onlookers left with a re-kindled faith. The participants went away unscorched, unburned — but on fire for the Lord.

Brother Everett Fraley tells a story of fire handling that happened near Big Stone Gap. "Nearly twenty years ago, we'd have a service in a home up there about once a week. They didn't have electricity; they had oil lamps. One night, the power of the Lord was really falling. The sister who owned the house was shouting (dancing and praising God while under the Spirit). She shouted over to one of those lamps, and her long hair went right down the chimney to the mantle. The flames were all in her hair, and it didn't scorch it one bit. Her hair stayed in there long enough for everybody to see it. She was dancing in the power of the Lord."

The devout handle fire by the same Spirit that anoints for the other signs and gifts. Clyde Ricker, who has often handled fire believes, "It takes a little more anointing to stick the flame to your flesh and just hold it there. But if God told me to stick it right in my face, I would."

This the youthful reverend did several times during an emotion-charged meeting at the Holiness Church of God in Jesus Name, Carson Springs. He strolled around the church for five minutes with his face totally engulfed in flames from a Coca-Cola bottle torch. Twice in this service the homemade torch was lit, both times by Brother Ricker. He jumped and he sang. His flesh didn't redden, and his heavy stubble of beard was not singed.

Sister Mary Bailey of Micco, West Virginia tells, "God has let me handle the fire three times without harm. And believe me, it's really a belssing to be able to handle the fire, to know that it has no power over you and it can't hurt you. It feels like a breeze coming by your hands and fingers. It's wonderful."

Sister Lida Davis doesn't know how many times she has done this. "A lot," she says. "I got healed one time through the anointing of the fire. I had those migraine headaches. I went to church in Nolan, West Virginia one night, and even the light hurt my eyes. The headache was terrible. I received the greatest anointing that night that I had ever had for the fire. I handled it. I came away from church healed, and I've not had those migraine headaches since."

"I'd love to handle fire," confesses Reverend Robert Grooms. "That's my desire. But every time I've touched it, it's always burned me." Brother Grooms, a most effective preacher, healer, and serpent handler, has firm ideas about the purpose of fire handling. "It's not a sign, but it shows what power God has. It shows what power He can give you to do these things with."

For this is good and acceptable in
the sight of God our Saviour.
1 Timothy, 2:3

Sister Thelma Whittaker holds the "fire bottle" to her hands during a recent service at the Full Gospel Jesus Church, Micco, West Virginia. "Oh! I feel just wonderful," explains Sister Thelma as the Holy Ghost manifested Itself in her. "Shun-mu-ma-ma-ma-ma-ma Oh! Praise God! It's the best blessing I've ever received in my life. Praise the Lord and hallelujah! You know, I had to tell my mother about this the other day, and she's an unbeliever. She got all over me. Praise the Lord! You know, God just gave me every kind of good Scriptures and things to give her." *Photo by Brother Dave Sexton.*

17

A Biblical Look—How It's Seen

But if ye believe not his writings,
how shall ye believe my words?
St. John, 5:47

All scripture is given by inspiration
of God, and is profitable for doctrine, for reproof, for correction,
for instruction in righteousness.
2 Timothy, 3:16

"We've got to take the Bible like it's written. If you're going to take part of it, and lay part of it down, you might as well let it all go. We need to abide in the Word and get the full meaning out of it," explains Reverend Robert Grooms. "The Word is spiritually understood. And without the Spirit of the Lord, nobody can understand it. You can read the Bible, and without the Spirit you can make many meanings out of it, many things. But with the Spirit of God, you get the true meaning. That's what's wrong with a lot of churches today. They don't have enough of the Spirit to understand what the Bible really means."

Robert Grooms feels he must be anointed by the Spirit before he can read the Scripture and get anything out of it. He gets "the best feeling" when reading it. Sometimes he'll be studying it and get so happy that he stops reading and starts singing. Sometimes Robert just sits down

155

and cries. This man quits reading the Bible if he does not become anointed. In such situations, the passages have no meaning whatsoever. It's just like reading the newspaper, and Robert feels it is a complete waste of time. In Brother Grooms' estimation, "If you've got the Spirit of God, you'll be able to understand the Bible. If you don't have the Spirit of God in you, you can't expect to understand a thing it says."

"Taking up the serpents is the Word of God just as much as laying hands on the sick," stresses Sister Ruth Dillon. "People love to lay hands on the sick, for they can't do no harm if they aren't healed. Know what I mean? But to take up serpents, one must live clean and be a *believer.* The five signs in Mark 16 are for the real believers. Thank God I'm a believer! God put me into this in 1948, and I've enjoyed it ever since. I wouldn't take nothing for my journey up until now. I'm too near home to give it up now."

"The Bible is the Word of God! I have faith in the Word of God. I believe this because the Spirit of God that's in me is the same Holy Ghost that was in the disciples back there that helped write the Bible." Reverend Willie Sizemore receives an anointing to preach, or he will let someone else do it. To him, the Bible is alive and very real. "I don't believe you can really preach until you've got the Holy Ghost. Because, if the Word was written by the prophets as they were moved on by the Holy Ghost, then it would take that same Holy Ghost to break the Word down to the people where they could see and understand it. It was written and inspired by God. I believe it has to be read and preached with the inspiration of God, or the Holy Ghost. When I search and read the scriptures under God's anointing, the Spirit moves on me and makes His Word come alive."

"The Bible was written by holy men of God. They were inspired by the Holy Ghost," says Sister Thelma Whittaker. "None of the Bible can possibly be wrong. I don't think God would have put 'they *shall* take up serpents' in His holy book if it didn't belong in there. After all, I don't think anyone can deny those are the words of Jesus."

"I didn't see taking up serpents when I first got right with the Lord. I had read it in the Bible, but I had to pray for a sign to show me it was right. I asked God to have one brought to the church." John Wayne Brown came into the faith approximately six years ago. "We were having a service one night. A little girl walked outside the door. There was a copperhead crawling in as she was going out. It had come from the nearby woods. Brother Jimmy Ray Williams went and got the serpent and handled it. I then knew by the witness of the Holy Ghost it was right. So I prayed that the Lord would let me do that, too, and He did!"

"They stand up and say Mark, 16:17 and 18 ought to be torn out of the Bible, that it don't belong in there," preaches Pastor Al Ball. "Amen, I would like to know what they think about Exodus, 4:4, Job, 26:13; Luke, 10:19; and Acts, 28—they mention handling serpents. I

Touch not mine anointed, and do
my prophets no harm.
1 Chronicles, 16:22

Reverend Alfred Ball calmly taking up a mass of serpents. "I don't try to prove my faith by picking up these serpents. I don't have to prove it, but the Spirit leads me to take them up. When God says, 'You do that,' or I think it's God, I immediately go to the Bible and see if there's any Scripture that says you are to do it. If there's not, then I simply don't do it."
Photo by the authors.

wonder if they feel these verses belong in the Bible? We always urge people to find a church that teaches the scriptures. We never ask anybody to blindly believe anything we can't back up with Bible scripture. God is just everything to me."

"When I pray to get victory over the serpent, to handle them, I'll wait until that certain feeling comes over me," tells Billy Jay Forrester. "It's hard to explain, but I want to move faster. I want to obey God and do His bidding. When I ask Him to let me do it, I want to get up right then and move and do it. Why do I want to? Because it's in the Bible. I believe, if unbelievers come hard against any of the other four signs, like they do taking up serpents, God'll anoint someone, and that sign will come out strong."

"I've never taken up serpents in church, but I have taken them up," expounds Brother Ralph Eslinger. "I can't find it nowhere in the Bible where it says to box up a bunch of serpents and carry them into a House of God. It says, 'These signs shall follow them that believe.' If I

Neither let us tempt Christ as
some of them also tempted, and
were destroyed of serpents.
1 Corinthians, 10:9

Brother Dewey Chafin of Jolo, West Virginia. This man has been bitten 56 times. "Jesus spoke the words. They are exactly as Jesus said them" argues Dewey in defense of Mark, 16:17-18. "Jesus said it Himself. They can't just take it out of the Bible. I don't think God would want us to do it if it were wrong. If it was wrong, God wouldn't have left it in the Bible. He don't ever lead us wrong."
Photo by the authors.

preach and teach that, some sinner-boy will bring in one, and God'll give me power over it. They sure don't have to be boxed up. The more you obey God and the more you walk after His commandments, the better blessing you receive. God can then do more for you, because you love Him and you obey Him. If God tells you to do something, and you don't do it, you'd just as well watch out for a whipping. This is all in the scripture."

"Amen. God don't just handle serpents. *I can preach the Word of God without handling serpents.* Amen, praise the Lord. But handling serpents *is still* the Word of God. Amen. When they come our way, in season, amen, it's the Word of God, ain't it?" Bishop Kelly Williams preached to a packed church. He was accompanied by sporadic words and nods of agreement from many enthusiastic members of the congregation. Some laced his sermon with an almost endless variety of tongues, as the Spirit moved on them. "Job said, 'my God can do anything.' Amen! Praise the Lord! Ain't that right? He's our God. And listen, that's why Job found favor in God's sight. Because he said, 'my God can do anything.' Amen. Our God *can* do anything, praise the Lord, *anything.* He can *heal* anything. Praise God for each and everyone of you tonight. Praise the Lord. Praise Him for this service. And praise Him for the Spirit we already found here tonight."

These sincere Holiness people are involved in a constant struggle for their right to perform the five scriptural signs as they see them. Everything from state laws to city ordinances are enacted to harass and prevent them. Yet, they seek to be permitted continuance of their unusual practices because "it's Bible." It is certainly not because they have gotten together, labeled themselves a church, and want to do something way-out.

"I believe you have the right to do anything God tells you to do inside the lids of that Bible. If they ask us why we take up serpents, we can turn to Mark, 16:18 and read it to them," explains Brother Robert Fraley. But he strongly feels it is wrong to hide behind the cry of religious freedom when a church sanctions marijuana smoking, human or animal sacrifice, and other unscriptural practices. These things, in his estimation, need to be emphatically stopped "because they are not in the Bible. The first question put to them should be, 'Can you turn in the Bible and find a scripture for smoking pot?' If it was in the Bible, 'They shall smoke pot,' I believe they've got a right to do it."

"God's works are holy works. God's people are holy people. If something's not in the Bible, we wouldn't do it," Sister Mary Bailey softly explains. "If the Word of God says to do something, I believe then that we had better do it. We better always obey the Word of God. Some say the sixteenth chapter of Mark doesn't really belong in the Bible. Those were words spoken by Jesus. It *does* belong in the Bible. And they can't take it out. They can't ignore it. Something like smoking marijuana is not the workings of God. It's *not* one of His signs. It's not in the scriptures. Marijuana smoking is a thing of the world. It is something that belongs to the devil. And God's people don't mess around with anything belonging to the devil."

The Bible provides these Christians with concrete guidelines for their entire lives — not just their worship habits. It dictates that they dress modestly. Most believe this means not too flashy, but not too drab, either. The women generally wear no make-up, jewelry, or slacks. Their dresses are normally below the knee or to the ankle. The men wear sport shirts and slacks, jeans, overalls, or a suit and tie.

The Bible gives them all the rules they live by.

"We were at a tent meeting about ten years ago, and a prophecy came through Dewey Cooper, the preacher. It came through about my hair. He told me to let my hair grow, to never cut it. He said as my hair got longer, I would get more power of God — the power would come. That has come to pass."

Sister Eunice Ball sincerely believes she must always leave her hair long. She feels she'd never have a chance again if it were to be cut. "The Bible plainly speaks that it's wrong. It says a woman's hair is her glory. One place it says if she be shorn, she might as well be shaven. In other words, if you cut it a little, you might as well shave it all off. I don't cut mine for any reason. That's one thing I wouldn't ever do — cut my hair!"

The Bible offers these fundamentalists a knowledge of and a closeness to their Heavenly Father. "You know where you stand with God," says Brother Ralph Spence, a profound man of unusually deep spiritual understanding. "I know when I'm walking close to God and when I'm trailing behind."

Why is the Bible not just a best-selling history book? Reverend Richard Williams had a ready answer. "The Bible is the only book in the world that is fulfilling itself everyday. For ages, people have done what it said they would do. People today are continuing to do what the Bible says they will do."

Although this religion is based on the Bible "from Genesis to Revealation," the members are called upon most often to defend the five signs in Mark. The sixty-sixth chapter of Isaiah, as explained by Richard Williams, reveals another purpose for serpent handling. "To me, handling a serpent is just a milestone to God. In the beginning, man had dominion over all things — lions, tigers, all the fowls of the air and the beasts of the earth. He had dominion over all of them. And I say that the real church is going to come back to that dominion. The serpents to us are just a stepping stone. If we continue to know the Lord in this way, it'll only be a matter of time 'til we'll be able to handle or play with anything."

Brother Ralph Spence agrees. "If we were to stay in the spiritual state all the time, that we are in when the anointing is upon us, we would be back in the state that Adam was before he sinned. Through Christ, we will gain this back."

Besides the idea that the last few verses in the book of Mark should not be in the Bible at all, there is another prevailing argument. That is, the five signs were given to the apostles for them and them alone. These signs are said to have served their purposes for the disciples, but are totally meaningless today. Brother Richard Williams' counter point to this theory is a lucid capsulization of the Holiness serpent handling beliefs.

"Jesus told the apostles, 'Go ye into all the world and preach the Gospel to every creature.' All He did there was tell them to preach. 'He that believeth and is baptized shall be saved.' Believeth what? Believeth the Gospel those boys preached! 'These signs shall follow . . .' Who, the apostles? It didn't say that. '. . . them that believe.' Believe what? Believe the Gospel! The five signs were made for *everyone* who believes the Gospel.

"We don't base our beliefs just on the signs. We base them on the man Jesus."

Appendix I

> ... I have set before thee an open door ... for
> thou hast kept my word and hast not denied my name.
>   Revelation, 2:8

> Jesus saith unto him, I am the way, the truth, and
> the life; no man cometh unto the Father, but by me.
>   John, 14:6

Richard Lee Williams of Hilliard, Ohio, was a child of God who died for his beliefs and for the Gospel.

On Tuesday, April 2, 1974, Richard was conducting revival services at the Full Gospel Jesus Church in Kistler, West Virginia. He and others handled a giant diamondback rattlesnake and had "perfect victory" over it. When the rattler had been put back in its box, Richard pointed at it and said, *"That serpent is here tonight for a purpose."*

At approximately 8:30 p.m., Reverend Williams returned to the box and reached in for the vicious reptile. The snake was barely in his grasp, when, with a lightning movement, it struck him on the palm of his left hand. He dropped the serpent and it fell onto its back in the box. Richard quickly went for it again. This time, in a flash of fury, the lethal fangs pierced the artery in his wrist. Blood spurted in all directions.

With a handkerchief wrapped around his wrist to inhibit the blood flow, the handsome blond preacher took the microphone. He spoke a few words of encouragement and reassurance to the breathless congregation, then went to the nearby home of Estle Evans, a church member. There, the saints prayed fervently for their beloved striken brother.

The arm swelled to a grotesque size and shape. The skin burst inside the elbow area. The pain must have been intense. Yet, he radiated a calm serenity and never once complained or cried out. His faith was strengthened with every throb, every pang — Richard Lee Williams never wavered. Near the end, Richard, at peace with himself, smiled, lovingly kissed his father, and said, "Well Dad, don't worry about me now. I wouldn't miss this chance to take a journey with the Lord for anything in the world." Through it all, he seemed to know it was his time.

One month before, a number of the faithful had prophesied a death "in service." Richard's mother-in-law, Carrie Cline, had recently dreamed of seeing him lying in a casket. Around 3:00 p.m., April 3, 1974, Richard Lee Williams quietly took his last breath.

> Precious in the sight of the Lord is the death of his saints.
> Psalms, 116:15

The fiery young preacher was only thirty-three years old. Jesus Christ was thirty-three when He was hammered to the cross on Calvary's hill. Richard Williams had a short but effective and far-reaching ministry. He was an evangelist, a teacher, and a diligent worker in the signs. His faith gave him a new life. He has given his life for that faith.

> 'Are ye able,' said the Master, 'To be crucified with Me?'
> 'Yea,' the conquering Christians answered, 'To the death
> we follow thee.'

But watch thou in all things, endure afflictions, do the work of an evangelist, make full proof of thy ministry. For I am now ready to be offered, and the time of my departure is at hand. I have fought a good fight, I have finished my course, I have kept the faith: Henceforth there is laid up for me a crown of righteousness, which the Lord, the righteous Judge, shall give me at that day: and not to me only, but unto all them also that love his appearing.

2 Timothy, 4:5 — 8

Appendix II

Let the word of Christ dwell in you
... in psalms, and hymns, and spirit—
ual songs, singing with grace in
your hearts to the Lord.
                              Colossians, 3:16

... go about the city ... make sweet
melody, sing many songs, that thou
mayest be remembered.
                              Isaiah, 23:16

A. FAVORITE SONGS SUNG DURING SERVICES

Music is a major part of the Holiness worship services. Guitars, electric and straight, tambourines, drums, and cymbals are standard instruments. There are usually a few regular singers from the church's congregation, but anyone who feels led by the Lord to sing a special message is warmly welcomed.

Reverend Alfred Ball, of the Holiness Church of God in Jesus Name, Carson Springs, Tennessee, organized a travelling singing group called the All for Jesus Singers. His husky-voiced young wife, Sister Eunice, is the lead singer, who, along with Alfred, plays a straight guitar. They go to serpent handling and other churches throughout the Southeast, playing and singing their unique style of mountain gospel rock and blues. The demand for them is growing as word is spread about Brother Al's dynamic evangelistic message and the group's foot-stomping, hand-clapping, tear-jerking, almost country-western way with a song.

Thus far, the All for Jesus Singers are unrecorded professionally. Few outside the isolated church circles they have played for have had the unequalled enjoyment of listening to their original approach. Much of their music is the old-time songs of fundamental faith. Sister Eunice has written several songs, and many are "made up as you go."

Following are some of the favorite songs, many of which have been handed down through the generations. No matter who is singing or playing, the music of the little country churches has a distinct flavor, unlike any heard anywhere else in the nation.

Darkest Hours

I walked down many roads in my lifetime,
Not knowing what my life held for me.
Troubles come, couldn't find no answer,
But I found Jesus in my darkest hours.

Chorus:
I found Him on a mountain top, in valleys so low,
And when my burdens got heavy, I knew where to go.
Trials came and no one seemed to care,
But I found Jesus in my darkest hours.

Oh, there'll be mountains to climb, valleys to go through
And there'll be burdens that we will have to bear.
Your friends will be few, when there were so many.
Yet, Jesus was there in my darkest hours.

Written by Sister Eunice Ball, Holiness Church of God in Jesus Name, Carson Springs, Tennessee.

Run a Little Harder

Chorus:
Run a little harder, if you want to go home.
You've got to fight a battle before you're strong.
Going along in Jesus name — He's still the mighty God,
No, He never changed.

Persecutions coming every day,
Then we know just what the Lord doth say.

Trials come on every hand.
Jesus gonna lead me to the promised land.

When you repent of all your sins,
Then a whole new life begins.
Go down to the water in Jesus Name — He's still the mighty God,
No, Ne never changed.

When I get to heaven, gonna look around
I'll put on my robe and I'll put on my crown.
I'll walk on the streets that are made of gold,
Live in a land where milk and honey flows.

Holy, Holy, Holy

Chorus:
Well, holy, holy, holy, and that's all right,
Well, holy, holy, holy, and that's all right,
Holy, holy, holy, and that's all right.
Oh, if you're living holy that's all right.

They call us holy rollers, but that's all right,
They call us holy rollers, but that's all right,
They call us holy rollers, but that's all right.
Oh, if you're living holy that's all right.

They say we're of the devil, but that's all right,
They say we're of the devil, but that's all right,
They say we're of the devil, but that's all right.
Oh, if you're living holy that's all right.

They call us Jesus only, but that's all right,
They call us Jesus only, but that's all right,
They call us Jesus only, but that's all right.
Oh, if you're living holy that's all right.

They call us serpent handlers, but that's all right,
They call us serpent handlers, but that's all right,
They call us serpent handlers, but that's all right.
Oh, if you're living holy that's all right.

They say we've all gone crazy, but that's all right,
They say we've all gone crazy, but that's all right,
They say we've all gone crazy, but that's all right.
Oh, if you're living holy, that's all right.

They call us the tongue gang, but that's all right,
They call us the tongue gang, but that's all right,
They call us the tongue gang, but that's all right.
Oh, if you're living holy that's all right.

An original song by members of various serpent handling churches throughout the Southeast. Given to the authors by Sister Eunice Ball. Holiness Church of God in Jesus Name, Carson Springs, Tennessee.

Zion, Oh Zion

Chorus:
Oh, Zion, oh, Zion
What's the matter now?
Oh, Zion, oh, Zion,
What's the matter now?

We used to sing and shout,
What's the matter now?
We used to sing and shout,
What's the matter now?

We used to speak in tongues,
What's the matter now?
We used to speak in tongues,
What's the matter now?

We used to pray for the sick,
What's the matter now?
We used to pray for the sick,
What's the matter now?

We used to cast out devils,
What's the matter now?
We used to cast out devils,
What's the matter now?

We used to take up serpents,
What's the matter now?
We used to take up serpents,
What's the matter now?

We used to love our brothers,
What's the matter now?
We used to love our brothers,
What's the matter now?

We used to believe the Bible,
What's the matter now?
We used to believe the Bible,
What's the matter now?

*An original song. Author unknown. Courtesy of Sister Eunice Ball,
Holiness Church of God in Jesus Name, Carson Springs, Tennessee.*

God Gave Me A Light

Chorus:
God gave me a light, and told me to let it shine.
God gave me a light, and told me to let it shine.
God gave me a light, and told me to let it shine.
Let it shine, let it shine, let it shine.

He saved this soul of mine, and I'm gonna let it shine.
He saved this soul of mine, and I'm gonna let it shine.
He saved this soul of mine, and I'm gonna let it shine.
Let it shine, let it shine, let it shine.

He gave me the Holy Ghost, and told me to let it shine.
He gave me the Holy Ghost, and told me to let it shine.
He gave me the Holy Ghost, and told me to let it shine.
Let it shine, let it shine, let it shine.

He healed this body of mine, and I'm gonna let it shine.
He healed this body of mine, and I'm gonna let it shine.
He healed this body of mine, and I'm gonna let it shine.
Let it shine, let it shine, let it shine.

Been baptized in His name, and I'm gonna let it shine.
Been baptized in His name, and I'm gonna let it shine.
Been baptized in His name, and I'm gonna let it shine.
Let it shine, let it shine, let it shine.

*An original song by members of various serpent handling churches.
Given to the authors by Sister Eunice Ball, Holiness Church of God in
Jesus Name, Carson Springs, Tennessee.*

Wading Through Deep Waters

Chorus:
I've been wading through deep waters trying to get home.
I've been wading through deep waters trying to get home.

I've been wading through deep waters, wading through deep waters,
I've been wading through deep waters trying to get home.

I'm gonna see the One who saved me, when I get home.
I'm gonna see the One who saved me, when I get home.
I'm gonna see the One who saved me, see the One who saved me,
I'm gonna see the One who saved me, when I get home.

All my sickness will be over, when I get home.
All my sickness will be over, when I get home.
All my sickness will be over, all my sickness will be over,
All my sickness wil be over, when I get home.

I'm gonna eat at a welcome table, when I get home.
I'm gonna eat at a welcome table, when I get home.
I'm gonna eat at a welcome table, eat at a welcome table,
I'm gonna eat at a welcome table, when I get home.

All my troubles will be over, when I get home.
All my troubles will be over, when I get home.
All my troubles will be over, trouble will be over,
All my troubles will be over, when I get home.

I'm gonna see my Jesus, when I get home.
I'm gonna see my Jesus, when I get home.
I'm gonna see my Jesus, gonna see my Jesus,
I'm gonna see my Jesus, when I get home.

*An original song. Author unknown. Courtesy of Sister Eunice Ball,
Holiness Church of God in Jesus Name, Carson Springs, Tennessee.*

Keeping Me Alive

Chorus:
Well, it's all over me, and it's keeping me alive,
Keeping me alive, keeping me alive.
Well, it's all over me, and it's keeping me alive,
Jesus is keeping me alive.

Well, I prayed it down from Heaven, and it's keeping me alive,
Keeping me alive, keeping me alive.
Well, I prayed it down from Heaven, and it's keeping me alive,
Jesus is keeping me alive.

Well, it's coming down from Heaven, and it's keeping me alive,
Keeping me alive, keeping me alive.

Well, it's coming down from Heaven, and it's keeping me alive,
Jesus is keeping me alive.

Oh, I feel it in my bones, and it's keeping me alive,
Keeping me alive, keeping me alive.
Oh, I feel it in my bones, and it's keeping me alive,
Jesus is keeping me alive.

It's the Holy Ghost and fire, and it's keeping me alive,
Keeping me alive, keeping me alive.
It's the Holy Ghost and fire, and it's keeping me alive
Jesus is keeping me alive.

It makes the devil mad, but it's keeping me alive,
Keeping me alive, keeping me alive.
It makes the devil mad, but it's keeping me alive,
Jesus is keeping me alive.

It makes me sing and shout, and it's keeping me alive
Keeping me alive, keeping me alive.
It makes me sing and shout, and it's keeping me alive,
Jesus is keeping me alive.

It makes me speak in tongues, and it's keeping me alive,
Keeping me alive, keeping me alive.
It makes me speak in tongues, and it's keeping me alive
Jesus is keeping me alive.

An original song. Author unknown. Courtesy of Sister Eunice Ball, Holiness Church of God in Jesus Name, Carson Springs, Tennessee.

I Believe There's A Heaven

I believe there's a Heaven. I believe there's wrong and right.
I believe there's a Saviour. I pray day and night.
I know for sure there is a God, and this is true.

If you, a sinner, keep giving excuses for refusing to see the light
They say there's so many religions that they can't all be right.
They say they can't be holy enough and with a troubled soul,
Well, I haven't got much learning, but there's one thing that I know.

There are people who go out dancing in the jump-joint every night.
They say if you don't overdo it, a little bit's all right.
They say they only go to see, but I know it's a fact
That you can't go down the chimney without getting a little black.

There are so many people, and I know they're very wrong.
And if they keep on sinning, their religion can't be strong.
I know there's lots of hypocrites, and there's one thing I've found,
If a sinner can't climb higher, he will try to pull you down.

An original song. Author unknown. Sand Hill Church of God in Jesus Name. Courtesy of Sister Bea Eslinger.

B. POEMS BY A MOUNTAIN PREACHER

Ralph Eslinger is a Tennesseean who loves God, his church, and his mountains. He finds it impossible to separate the three. He worships God as freely from a mountaintop as from a church house. Yet, he attends services regularly and often preaches at the House of Prayer in Morristown, or the Holiness Church of God in Jesus Name, Carson Springs.

Ralph, a giant of a man whose gentleness matches his size, periodically goes off into the mountains to be alone with the Lord. Surrounded by the calm serenity of nature, he communes closely with God. This man will often be filled with the Holy Ghost and handle coals from his camp fire or take up a meandering rattlesnake. Or, perhaps, he will write. Big Ralph is a farmer with little schooling, but he is frequently moved to write about his religious feelings. The simplicity of a child, the purity of a Christian, and a deep love of God are warmly evident in the poems of this mountain preacher.

TEACH ME

Whin I GROW up AND BECOME A MAN
HELP ME LORd To UNdER STANd.
THE WAYS OF LiFE ANd WHERE iT BEGANS
how To REPEHT ANd BE BoRNEd AGAiN.
TEACH ME God To NEAL And PRAY
whin I GROW up I wiLL NEVER STRAY.
I WANT To LoVE my NABOR FRom dAY To dAY
And LET my LiTTLE Light SHiNE ALoNg
                              THE WAY.
TEACH ME God To do My BEST
  † No you CAN do THE REST.

I Am WEAK ANd you ARE STRoNg
  YOU CAN KEEP ME FRom ALL RoNg.
I hAVE SEEN So mANY FALL ALoNg THE WAY
hELPE ME NOT To Go ThAT A STBAY.
PLEASE God LENd ME A hELPiNG hANd
ANd LEAd ME To THE pROmi's LANd.
whin I giT THAiR I wiLL uNdER STANd
Whow I GROWED up ANd BECOME A MAN.

Ralph Eslinger

God's Church

PEOPLE COME FORM FAR And NEAR,
   To A LITTLE ChuRCh I LOLE So dEAR.
iT LiES in THE hART oF THE MounTAns
ho so hiGh,
   ThATS WhERE JESUS bLEEd And diEd.
hE ShEEd his BLood A BRod FoR mE,
   ThAT I may EVER LiLE I hopE To SEE.
I hopE To MEET him somE GLAd dAy,
   AT my JuAhEys End oR ALong THE WAy.
I whAnT To hEAR him sAy wiLL DohE
my ChiLD,
   TAKE youR REST FoR A LiTTLE WhiLE.

iT mAy BE BATTERd iT mAy bE SChoRnEd,
   buT iTS STood ThRouW THE RAin And STORm.
Whin God ToLD PETOR hE ToLD him WELL,
   ThE GATES oF hELL ShALL NoT PROLiLL.
SomE pEopLE BRAng ThAiR CAMERAS,
   SomE BRAng ThAiR CRoos,
SomE IVEh TRys To BRAng ThAiR BRoos.

whin God Comes Down in A miTy WAY,
THATS whin The deLiL BE gAins To Sw AY.

PEoPLE TRimBLE whin Thay hEAR ME SAY,
THAT WRITE SATioH WhERE hEAR To STAY.

This hEAR SERponT I hoLD in My hAnd,
THATS To REmind you SinnERS hES
King oF ThE LAnd.

iF you will LET him he will TAKE
youR hAnd,
And LEAd you To ThE PRomi's LAnd.

iF you WAnT To Go To hELAn you
goT To pAy THE CosT,
you GoT To ComE ThRoh JESuS ARE
you WilL EliER BE LosT.

you goT To REPEnT And BE BoRnEd AgAin,
To inTER inTo ThE pRomES LAnd.

whin you do you WilL unDER STAnd,
whEy I Took yEsuS By ThE hAnd.

Ralph Holinger

Appendix III

... when they persecute you in this
city, flee ye into another.
St. Matthew, 10:23

Be sober, be vigilant; because your
adversary the devil, as a roaring
lion, walketh about, seeking whom
he may devour.
2 Peter, 5:8

SOUTHEASTERN STATE LAWS REGARDING SERPENT HANDLING

ALABAMA

CHAPTER 75A.

Snakes and Reptiles

Sec.
419(1).   [Superseded].
419(2).   Displaying etc., poisonous snakes and reptiles.
419(3).   Same; penalty.

†419(1): Superseded by †† 419(2) and 419(3) of this title.

Note.—The Superseded section was codified from Acts 1950, 5th Ex. Sess., p. 91, appvd. Oct. 31, 1950.

†419(2). Displaying, etc., poisonous snakes and reptiles.—It shall be unlawful for any person, or persons, to display, exhibit, handle or use any poisonous or dangerous snake or reptile in such a manner as to endanger the life or health of any person. (1953, p. 684, † 1, appvd. Sept. 3, 1953.)

Constitutionality.—This section does not violate either the federal or
state constitutional guarantees of freedom of religion. Hill v. State,
38 Ala. App. 404, 88 So. (2d) 880.

The violation of the statute is complete if the life or health of one
person is endangered and the fact that the affidavit sets out that the
offense was committed with reference to affiant and various other
persons does not make it necessary for the state to prove that both
affiant and various other people were endangered in their lives and
health. Hill v. State, 38 Ala. App. 404, 88 So. (2d) 880.

Indictment.—This section, which became effective on Sept. 3, 1953,
changed the offense covered by former † 419(1) from a felony to a
misdemeanor. Thus an indictment charging a violation of this section
within 12 months of an affidavit sworn to on June 14, 1954, but
which failed to state the date of the offense, was subject to
demurrer; however, the indictment was not void, and defendant was
not entitled to a motion to exclude the evidence and for his
discharge made at the conclusion of the state's evidence. Hill v. State,
38 Ala. App. 404, 88 So. (2d) 880.

†419(3). Same; penalty.—Any person violating the provisions of section 419(2) shall be guilty of a misdemeanor and punished by a fine of not less than fifty ($50.00) dollars nor more than one hundred and fifty ($150.00) dollars, or by confinement in jail not exceeding six months, or by both such fine and imprisonment, in the discretion of the court. (1953, p. 684, † 2, appvd. Sept. 3, 1953.)

FLORIDA[1]

372.86 Possessing, exhibiting poisonous or venomous reptile; license required.—No person, firm or corporation shall keep, possess or exhibit any poisonous or venomous reptile without first having obtained a special permit or license therefor from the Florida game and fresh water fish commission as herein provided.

History.—†1, ch. 28263, 1953.

---

1. Venomous reptile license can be seen at the end of this section.

372.87 License fee; renewal, revocation.—The Florida game and fresh water fish commission is hereby authorized and empowered to issue a license or permit for the keeping, possessing or exhibiting of poisonous or venomous reptiles, upon payment of an annual fee of five dollars and upon assurance that all of the provisions of ††372.86-372.91 and such other reasonable rules and regulations as said commission may prescribe will be fully complied with in all respects. Such permit may be revoked by the Florida game and fresh water fish commission upon violation of any of the provisions of ††372.86-372.91 or upon violation of any of the rules and regulations prescribed by said commission relating to the keeping, possessing and exhibiting of any poisonous and venomous reptiles. Such permits or licenses shall be for an annual period to be prescribed by the said commission and shall be renewable from year to year upon the payment of said five dollars fee and shall be subject to the same conditions, limitations and restrictions as herein set forth.

History.—†2, ch. 28263, 1953.

372.88 Bond required, amount.—No person, party, firm or corporation shall exhibit to the public either with or without charge, or admission fee any poisonous or venomous reptile without having first posted a good and sufficient bond in writing in the penal sum of one thousand dollars payable to the governor of the state, and his successors in office, conditioned that such exhibitor will indemnify and save harmless all persons from injury or damage from such poisonous or venomous reptiles so exhibited and shall fully comply with all laws of the state and all rules and regulations of the Florida game and fresh water fish commission governing the keeping, possessing or exhibiting of poisonous or venomous reptiles; provided, however, that the aggregate liability of the surety for all such injuries or damages shall, in no event, exceed the penal sum of said bond. The surety for said bond must be a surety company authorized to do business under the laws of the state or in lieu of such a surety, cash in the sum of one thousand dollars may be posted with the said commission to insure compliance with the conditions of said bond.

History.—†3, ch. 28263, 1953.

372.89 Safe housing required.—All persons, firms, or corporations licensed under this law to keep, possess or exhibit poisonous or venomous reptiles shall provide safe, secure and proper housing for said reptiles in cases, cages, pits or enclosures. It shall be unlawful for any person, firm or corporation, whether licensed hereunder or not, to keep, possess or exhibit any poisonous or venomous reptiles in any manner not approved as safe, secure and proper by the Florida game and fresh water fish commission.

History.—†4, ch. 28263, 1953; †1, ch. 57-415.

372.90 Transportation.—Poisonous or venomous reptiles may be transported only in the following fashion: The reptile, or reptiles shall be placed in a stout closely woven cloth sack, tied or otherwise secured. This sack shall then be placed in a box. The box shall be of strong material in solid sheets, except for small air holes, which holes shall be screened. Boxes containing poisonous or venomous snakes or other reptiles shall be prominently labeled "Danger—Poisonous Snakes" or "Danger—Poisonous Reptiles."

History.—†5, ch. 28263, 1953; †1, ch. 57-415.

372.901 Inspection.—Poisonous or venomous reptiles, held in captivity, shall be subject to inspection by an inspecting officer from the Florida game and fresh water fish commission. The inspecting officer shall determine whether the said reptiels are securely, properly and safely penned. In the event that the reptiles are not safely penned, the inspecting officer shall report the situation in writing to the person or firm owning the said reptiles. Failure of the owner or exhibitor to correct the situation within thirty days after such written notice shall be grounds for revocation of the license or permit of said owner or exhibitor.

History—†, ch. 57-415.

372.91 Opening cages, etc., housing poisonous or venomous reptiles.—No person except the licensee or his authorized employee shall open any cage, pit or other container which contains poisonous or venomous reptiles.

History.—†7, ch. 28263, 1953.

372.911 Penalty.—Any person violating any provision of this chapter shall be guilty of a misdemeanor of the second degree, punishable as provided in †775.082 or †775.083. The game and fresh water fish commission is authorized to offer rewards of up to five hundred dollars to any person furnishing information leading to the arrest and conviction of any person who has inflicted or attempted to inflict bodily injury upon any wildlife officer engaged in the enforcement of the provisions of this chapter or the rules and regulations of the game and fresh water fish commission.

History.—†2, ch. 57-415; †1, ch. 59-318, ch. 71-136.

372.92 Rules and regulations.—The Florida game and fresh water fish commission may prescribe such other rules and regulations as it may deem necessary to prevent the escape of poisonous and venomous reptiles, either in connection of construction of such cages or otherwise to carry out the intent of ††372.86-372.91.

STATE OF FLORIDA
GAME AND FRESH WATER FISH COMMISSION
TALLAHASSEE, FLORIDA

———

APPLICATION FOR LICENSE TO EXHIBIT
POISONOUS OR VENOMOUS REPTILES

———

DATE_____ , 19__

Game and Fresh Water Fish Commission
Tallahassee, Florida

Gentlemen:

I enclose herewith $5.00 in payment of License to Exhibit Poisonous or Venomous Reptiles under regulation prescribed by law and by rules and regulations of the Game and Fresh Water Fish Commission.

I hereby certify that I have posted a good and sufficient bond in the penal sum of $1000.00 payable to the Governor of the State of Florida, as provided by Section 372.88, Florida Statutes, and that a true and correct copy of this bond is attached.

License for license year 19__-19__and to expire June 30, 19__.

Signed _____

Street or RFD _____

P. O. Address _____

Age _____

GEORGIA

The state of Georgia has no statute which specifically addresses itself to, or forbids, the handling of poisonous or dangerous reptiles.[2]

KENTUCKY

437.060 [1267a-1] Use of reptiles in religious services.

Any person who displays, handles or uses any kind of reptiles in connection with any religious service or gathering shall be fined not less than fifty dollars nor more than one hundred dollars.

Constitutionality:
This act is constitutional. Lawson v. Com., 291 Ky. 437, 164 S.W. (2d) 972.

437.070 [1318] Arrest of clergyman while performing religious worship.

Any officer who arrests, or attempts to arrest, for any civil cause, any clergyman while he is publicly preaching or performing religious worship in any religious assembly shall be fined not less than ten nor more than fifty dollars.

NORTH CAROLINA

Article 55.

Handling of Poisonous Reptiles

†14-416. Handling of poisonous reptiles declared public nuisance and criminal offense.—The intentional exposure of human beings to contact with reptiles of a venomous nature being essentially dangerous and injurious and detrimental to public health, safety and welfare, the indulgence in and inducement to such exposure is hereby declared to be a public nuisance and a criminal offense, to be abated and punished as provided in this article. (1949, c.1084.)

†14-418. Prohibited handling of reptiles or suggesting or inducing others to handle.—It shall be unlawful for **any person** to intentionally handle any reptile of a poisonous nature whose venom is not removed,

---

2. Some communities have passed local ordinances.

by taking or holding such reptile in bare hands or by placing or holding such reptile against any exposed part of the human anatomy, or by placing their own or another's hand or any other part of the human anatomy in or near any box, cage, or other container wherein such reptile is known or suspected to be. It shall also be unlawful for any person to intentionally suggest, entice, invite, challenge, intimidate, exhort or otherwise induce or aid any person to handle or expose himself to any such poisonous reptile in any manner defined in this article. (1949, c. 1084, s.3.)

†14-419. Investigation of suspected violations; seizure and examination of reptiles; destruction or return of reptiles.—In any case in which any law-enforcement office has reasonable grounds to believe that any of the provisions of this article have been or are about to be violated, it shall be the duty of such officer and he is hereby authorized, empowered, and directed to immediately investigate such violation or impending violation and to forthwith seize the reptile or reptiles involved, and all such officers are hereby authorized and directed to deliver such reptiles to the respective county health authorities for examination and tests of such reptiles by such authorities or other qualified purpose of ascertaining whether said reptiles contain venom and are poisonous. If such health authorities, or other qualified authorities designated by them to make such examinations and tests, find that said reptiles are dangerously poisonous, it shall be the duty of the officers making the seizure, and they are hereby authorized and directed to forthwith destroy such reptiles; but if said health authorities, or other qualified authorities by them designated to make such examination and tests, find that the reptiles are not dangerously poisonous, and are not and cannot be harmful to human life, safety, health or welfare, then it shall be the duty of such officers to return the said reptiles to the person from whom they were seized. (1949, c. 1084, s. 4.)

†14-420. Arrest of persons violating provisions of article.—If the examination and tests made by the county health or other qualified authorities as provided herein show that such reptiles are dangerously poisonous, it shall be the duty of the officers making the seizure, in addition to destroying such reptiles, also to arrest all persons violating any of the provisions of this article. (1949, c. 1084, s. 5.)

†14-421. Exemptions from provisions of article.—This article shall not apply to the possession, exhibition, or handling of reptiles by employees or agents of duly constituted museums, laboratories, educational or scientific institutions in the course of their educational or scientific work. (1949, c. 1084, s. 6.)

†14-422. Violation made misdemeanor.—Any person violating any of the provisions of this article shall be guilty of a misdemeanor punishable by a fine not to exceed five hundred dollars ($500.00), imprisonment for not more then six months, or both. (1949, c. 1084, s. 7; 1969, c. 1224, s. 3.)

Editor's Note.—The 1969 amendment rewrote the provisions relating to punishment.

OHIO

The state of Ohio has no statute which specifically addresses itself to, or forbids, the handling of poisonous or dangerous reptiles.[3]

SOUTH CAROLINA

The state of South Carolina has no statute which specifically addresses itself to, or forbids, the handling of poisonous or dangerous reptiles.[4]

TENNESSEE

39-2208. Handling snakes so as to endanger life—Penalty.—It shall be unlawful for any person, or persons, to display, exhibit, handle or use any poisonous or dangerous snake or reptile in such a manner as to endanger the life or health of any person.

Any person violating the provisions of this section shall be guilty of a misdemeanor and punished by a fine of not less than fifty dollars ($50.00) nor more than one hundred and fifty dollars ($150), or by confinement in jail not exceeding six (6) months, or by both such fine and imprisonment, in the discretion of the court. [Acts 1947, ch. 89, ††1, 2; C. Supp. 1950, †11173.1 (Williams, ††11412.14, 11412.15).]

Comparative Legislation. Handling N. Car. Gen. Stat. 1943, ††14-416—snakes so as to endanger life: 14-422.

Ala. Code 1940, tit. 14, ††419(2), Va. Code 1950, †18-73. 419(3).

NOTES TO DECISIONS

Analysis
1. Constitutionality.
2. Purpose and policy.
3. Construction and interpretation.
4. Proof.

3. Some communities have passed local ordinances.
4. Ibid.

1. Constitutionality.

The provisions of this section prohibiting handling, exhibition and display of poisonous snakes does not violate the freedom of religious worship guaranteed by the state and federal constitutions. Harden v. State (1948), 188 Tenn. 17, 216 S. W. (2d) 708.

2. Purpose and Policy.

The language of this section is by necessary implication a legislative declaration that handling of a poisonous snake is dangerous to life and health.

3. Construction and Interpretation.

There are no exceptions from the provisions of this section. Harden v. State (1948), 188 Tenn. 17, 216 S. W. (2d) 708.

4. Proof.

In prosecution under this section the state was not required to show that venom pouch had not been removed from rattlesnake since it was an established fact that all rattlesnakes were poisonous hence it would be presumed that snake exhibited was not an exception. Harden v. State (1948), 188 Tenn. 17, 216 S. W. (2d) 708.

VIRGINIA

†18.1-72. Handling or using snakes so as to endanger human life or health.—It shall be unlawful for any person, or persons, to display, exhibit, handle or use any poisonous or dangerous snake or reptile in such a manner as to endanger the life or health of any person.

Any person violating the provisions of this section shall be guilty of a misdemeanor and punished by a fine of not less than fifty dollars nor more than one hundred and fifty dollars, or by confinement in jail not exceeding six months, or by both such fine and imprisonment. (Code 1950, †18-73; 1960, c. 358.)

WEST VIRGINIA

The state of West Virginia has no statute which specifically addresses itself to, or forbids, the handling of poisonous or dangerous reptiles.[5]

5. Some communities have passed local ordinances.

Appendix IV

For the Lord is our judge, the Lord
is our Lawgiver, the Lord is our
King; he will save us.
Isaiah, 33:22

There is one lawgiver, who is able
to save, and to destroy . . .
James, 4:12

SOUTHEASTERN STATE CONSTITUTIONAL
RELIGIOUS GUARANTEES

RELIGIOUS GUARANTEE
CONSTITUTION OF THE UNITED STATES OF AMERICA

Article I. Congress shall make no law respecting an establishment of religion, or prohibiting the free exercise thereof; or abridging the freedom of speech, or of the press; or the right of the people peaceably to assemble, and to petition the government for a redress of grievances.

RELIGIOUS GUARANTEES
SOUTHEASTERN STATE CONSTITUTIONS

ALABAMA

Section 3. Religious freedom. That no religion shall be established by law; that no preference shall be given by law to any religious sect, society, denomination, or mode of worship; that no one shall be compelled by law to attend any place of worship; nor to pay any tithes, taxes, or other rate for building or repairing any place of worship, or for maintaining any minister or ministry; that no religious test shall be required as a qualification to any office or public trust under this state; and that the civil rights, privileges, and capacities of any citizen shall not be in any manner affected by his religious principles.

FLORIDA

Section 5. Religious freedom; liberty of conscience; etc. The free exercise and enjoyment of religious profession and worship shall for-ever be allowed in this State, and no person shall be rendered incompetent as a witness on account of his religious opinions; but the liberty of conscience hereby secured shall not be so construed as to justify licentiousness or practices subversive of, or inconsistent with, the peace or moral safety of the State or society.

GEORGIA

Paragraph XIII. Religious opinions; liberty of conscience. No inhabitant of this State shall be molested in person or property, or prohibited from holding any public office, or trust, on account of his religious opinions; but the right of liberty of conscience shall not be so construed as to excuse acts of licentiousness, or justify practices inconsistent with the peace and safety of the State.

KENTUCKY

Section 5. Right of religious freedom. No preference shall ever be given by law to any religious sect, society or denomination; nor to any particular creed, mode of worship or system of ecclesiastical polity; nor shall any person be compelled to attend any place of worship, to contribute to the erection or maintenance of any such place, or to the salary or support of any minister of religion; nor shall any man be compelled to send his child to any school to which he may be conscientiously opposed; and the civil rights, privileges or capacities of no person shall be taken away, or in anywise diminished or enlarged, on account of his belief or disbelief of any religious tenet, dogma or teaching. No human authority shall, in any case whatever, control or interfere with the rights of conscience.

NORTH CAROLINA

Section 26. Religious liberty. All persons have a natural and inalienable right to worship Almighty God according to the dictates of their own consciences, and no human authority should, in any case whatever, control or interfere with the rights of conscience.

OHIO

Section 7. Rights of conscience; the necessity of religion and knowledge. All men have a natural and indefeasible right to worship Almighty God according to the dictates of their own conscience. No person shall be compelled to attend, erect, or support any place of worship, or maintain any form of worship, against his consent; and no preference shall be given, by law, to any religious society; nor shall any interference with the rights of conscience be permitted. No religious test shall be required, as a qualification for office, nor shall any person be incompetent to be a witness on account of his religious belief; but nothing herein shall be construed to dispense with oaths and affirmations. Religion, morality, and knowledge, however, being essential to good government, it shall be the duty of the General Assembly to pass suitable laws, to protect every religious denomination in the peaceable enjoyment of its own mode of public worship, and to encourage schools and the means of instruction.

SOUTH CAROLINA

Section 4. Religious worship; freedom of speech; petition. The General Assembly shall make no law respecting an establishment of religion or prohibiting the free exercise thereof, or abridging the freedom of speech or of the press; or the right of the people peaceably to assemble and to petition the Government or any department thereof for a redress of grievances.

TENNESSEE

Section 3. Right of worship free. That all men have a natural and indefeasible right to worship Almighty God according to the dictates of their own conscience; that no man can of right be compelled to attend, erect, or support any place of worship, or to maintain any minister against his consent; that no human authority can, in any case whatever, control or interfere with the rights of conscience; and that no preference shall ever be given, by law, to any religious establishment or mode of worship.

VIRGINIA

Section 16. Religious freedom. That religion or the duty which we owe to our Creator, and the manner of discharging it, can be directed only by reason and conviction, not by force or violence; and, therefore, all men are equally entitled to the free exercise of religion, according to the dictates of conscience; and that it is the mutual duty of all to practice Christian forbearance, love and charity towards each other.

WEST VIRGINIA

15. Religious freedom guaranteed. No man shall be compelled to frequent or support any religious worship, place or ministry whatsoever; nor shall any man be enforced, restrained, molested or burthened, in his body or goods or otherwise suffer, on account of his religious opinions or belief, but all men shall be free to profess, and, by argument, to maintain their opinions in matters of religion; and the same shall, in no wise, affect, diminish or enlarge their civil capacities; and the legislature shall not prescribe any religious test whatever, or confer any peculiar privileges or advantages on any sect or denomination, or pass any law requiring or authorizing any religious society, or the people of any district within this State, to levy on themselves, or others, any tax for the erection or repair of any house for public worship, or for the support of any church or ministry, but it shall be left free for every person to select his religious instructor, and to make for his support such private contract as he shall please.